THE RESTLESS GENERATION

The Restless Generation

A Crisis in Mobility

PATRICK RIVERS

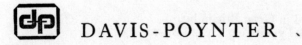

DAVIS-POYNTER

First published in 1972 by
Davis-Poynter Limited
Broadwick House Broadwick Street
London W1V 2AH

Copyright © 1972 by Patrick Rivers

ISBN 0 7067 0021 X

Printed in Great Britain by
Bristol Typesetting Co Ltd Bristol

FOR SHIRLEY

Contents

Acknowledgements

I AM indebted to many people and organizations for their help. It has taken many forms: information and ideas, encouragement and criticism, discussion, correspondence, and reading the many drafts – in some cases extracts, in others the whole typescript. Dr Mayer Hillman willingly performed all these tasks and more besides. In particular I should like to record my gratitude to Dr John Davoll, Professor John Kenneth Galbraith, Edward Goldsmith, Christine Hull, Brian Navin, John Ridley, J. Michael Thomson.

I should also like to record my appreciation to Kenneth Allsop, Max Boyd, Fred Brazier, Willie L. Brown, John Carter, Harry Chandler, Cal Cohn, William Cormack, Tony Dawe, Anne Donner, H. Whitney Ellsworth, Ian Fulton, Ghriam Grant, Hazel Henderson, Herbert L. Hiller, Mary Lee Hiller, Gerald Hoinville, William Hoppen, Colin Hutchinson, Theodore W. Kheel, Dr G. Mackay, Julian Mounter, William Osborn, Stephen Plowden, Dr Robert Rapoport, Arthur Reed, Jacquelin T. Robertson, Tim Rock, Angela Rooney, John Rowan, Professor Richard Scorer, Constantine Sidamon-Eristoff, Bryan Silcock, Goody L. Solomon, Alice Tepper, Sergio Viggiani, Professor C. Voûte, and H. F. Wallis.

I must also thank many organizations, including: The Automobile Association; British Overseas Airways Corporation; British Railways Board; Caribbean Travel Association Miami; The Conservation Society; Council for Economic Priorities, New York; Department of the Environment; Department of Trade and Industry; Department of Transportation, Washington, D.C.; Environmental Protection Agency, New York; Environmental Scientists' Consultancy, New Jersey; Federal Aviation Administration, Washington, D.C.; Institute of Petroleum; International Air Transport Association, Geneva; London Amenity and Transport Association; London Motorway Action Group; Metra Consulting Group Ltd; National Association of Railroad Passengers, Washington, D.C.; National Coalition on the Transportation Crisis, Washington, D.C.; National Council on Inland Transport; New Scotland Yard; Noise Abatement Society; Office of Midtown Planning and Development, New York; Pedestrians' Association for Road Safety; Royal Society for the Prevention of Accidents; Society of Motor Manufacturers and Traders; Sunday Times Editorial Library; Transport Administration Commission, New York; Thomas Cook & Sons Ltd; UNESCO Division of Application of Social Services, Paris; UNESCO Office of the Chief Mission, Indonesia; World Council of Churches, Geneva.

I hasten to add that the inclusion of any person or organization in this list of acknowledgements does not necessarily indicate that they agree with the views expressed in this book.

Preface

In a way this book was born twenty years ago. I was farming then and observing the unpleasant things that were
happening as the worlds of man and nature increasingly
diverged. In time I wrote about some of them as journalist
and editor, but not until I found myself heading a small
pressure group did I sense the gulf between professional
detachment and personal involvement. When a handful of
us won the first round against a motorway's grave mischief,
I realized that the effects of greed and mindlessness were
not irreversible: they simply thrived on passive acceptance.
From loss of wilderness to loss of homes, the effects could
be checked by awareness and action. And that is what *The
Restless Generation* is about.

1 Mobility: the New God

This is the age of the mobility explosion: the time of the 'Great Conspiracy' between Government and business. Together these two major forces have exploited man's inherent drives and created the world's largest, fastest growing and most potentially destructive industry – Mobility. In both Britain and the USA up to one-fifth of national output is in one way or another involved in moving goods and people from one place to another. The United States of America alone spends over $160 billion* dollars a year directly on transport, officially estimated to cause half the country's tonnage of air pollution.

Once the man-made world was richly varied. When movement from town to town, country to country was slow, costly and hazardous, each place developed in its own distinctive way . . . customs, costumes, art and architecture. As the means to travel gradually improved, contact between places became easier and the differences began to disappear. Now that cheap mobility is the new cult, variety has become one of the first major casualties. Destinations draw closer, but their worth diminishes.

Apparently man needs constant stimulation, competition and a sense of achievement if he is to feel fulfilled; as he satisfies each new desire so he looks for another. The modern industrial state feeds avidly on this need for change, transmuting it into a desire for industry and growth, channelling resources where they will create most distraction, rather than where they will fill the basic needs of a humane, pleasant environment. People deprived of such needs have

* A billion throughout refers to 1,000 million

13

greatest need for escapism. The industries that keep man and his materials on the move have grown rapidly as a result of this economic perversion – in particular those that produce both car and aircraft.

The car has profoundly changed our lives, whether we own one or not. And now, heedless of American experience, Britain is creating a car-dominated society, forgetful that, although most people need independent travel, nearly forty million are without exclusive use of a car – and any change can only be gradual. If the car has become the supreme personal status symbol, the aircraft has become a *national* status symbol; the show-piece of every country that has arrived. Yet so far we have experienced only a glimmer of the destructive forces it is capable of unleashing on our persons and our environment. Born eighty-five years ago, the car has had a full life, but there are signs that it is bringing its own decline – if not its death. The aircraft in contrast has scarcely arrived. Before World War Two it was still a novelty and you could dine out for days with a gripping account of your long, hazardous journey. Now, the aircraft industry, cosseted and subsidized, already offers fast, cheap, uneventful travel to anywhere. But such a miracle can easily mask the costs and nuisances: fifteen million British citizens already suffer aircraft noise. Airports are hungry for land, and homes are endangered. It has been estimated that Britain has more airfields to the square mile than any other nation-state – with the possible exception of Singapore. Yet this is only the beginning. The Jumbo Jet can carry more that 450 people, and planes to carry 1,000 or more are planned. Throughout the world, passenger miles flown have increased fourfold in the last ten years. On past trends, and despite the recession of the early seventies, air traffic is expected to increase to around *fifteen times* its present level in the next 30 years.

Growth of this magnitude depends on a supply of two special kinds of passenger: businessmen and tourists. As the world shrinks into one mass market for the multinational companies and property developers, the same goods, airports, motorways and buildings appear everywhere. In the places where businessmen have yet to make their mark, tourism does the same work with equal precision. Nations seeking economic advancement are abandoning the cultural traditions which kept them stable, imitating the Western industrial élite in the attempt to catch up with them.

The history of mankind is studded with migrations: at first hesitant and often unsuccessful shifts of population; bolder, more ambitious and more independent of family and tribe as man mastered cart, ship and machine. In time he set up new centres of population across the globe. When man set about subduing the Earth in earnest his numbers were few. At the time he set sail for the New World the population of the world was about 500 million. So long as his resources were meagre his errors were quickly healed by nature. So long as he could find fresh land, old pastures had time to recover. If he doubted the rightness of his mission, he was reassured from beyond: 'And God said Let Us make man in Our image, after Our likeness: and let him have dominion over the fish of the sea, and over the fowl of the air, and over cattle, and over every creeping thing that creepeth upon earth . . . and God said unto them, Be fruitful, and multiply, and replenish the Earth and subdue it'. Thus the concept of stewardship conferred respectability on man's activities. If at times he made mistakes they could be shrugged off as the price of necessary experiment. It was not easy to assume the mantle of God overnight, and in a bountiful and seemingly inexhaustible world the odd mistake was surely forgivable. But he has overlooked at least one divine tenet: he has forgotten to replenish. Now to re-create even a part of what he has destroyed will consume many times the effort he has so far expended. Today the population of the world is 3.6 billion, due to double in the next thirty years and set for 15.5 billion a century hence: well over four times the present population.

Man's effect on the planet – its climate, soil, flora and fauna – approaches the magnitude of another ice age, and the planet is reacting at an alarming rate. Air, land, rivers, lakes and oceans are seriously polluted and dates can now be charted when many of the world's vital resources will be mined and dissipated. Man is sacrificing other life forms – animals, birds, fish, forests and flowers – yet the world we know can survive without General Motors, but not without green plants. At last man is beginning to see he has a problem, part of which is that he is running out of space and has nowhere else to go. The realization of the impossibility of infinite growth in a finite world is cascading into contemporary thought, and this overdue awakening has severe economic implications. Yet the economies of industrial societies depend as much upon the concept of an inexhaustible world as upon man remaining a creature of inexhaustible desires.

A human being is the world's most complex organism, slow growing and needing maximum care. With too many on earth, too few will grow to know what it is to be a complete, fulfilled person. Instead, more will grow up ill-nourished in poverty and disease, among racial strife, in noisy polluted cities, and under the growing threat of nuclear war. Our species has reached the point in its evolution where each extra child born reduces the possibilities of happiness for those already here. This important truth was eloquently stated over 100 years ago by an obscure mathematician called William Forster Lloyd, and recently reported by Garrett Hardin in *Science*. Lloyd used an analogy of a common pasture (or 'commons'), where each herdsman would try to keep as many cattle as possible. So long as wars, poaching and disease keep numbers below the maximum the pasture will carry, all are fed and the pasture does not suffer. When these undesirables are no longer present, however, the inherent 'logic of the commons' remorselessly generates tragedy. As a rational being, each herdsman seeks to maximize his gain and adds first one animal and then others. Each fresh animal means a positive gain of one to him and a loss to his neighbours of a fraction of one. Each extra animal added by his neighbour similarly means a fractional loss to him. But he has too many neigh-bours; therefore the combined effect is to create a far greater loss to him than will accrue from his own, now undernourished animals. Each individual becomes locked in a system that compels him to increase without limit – within an environment that is limited.

The 'tragedy of the commons' has a direct relevance to today's economic and social problems. Particularly relevant is the question of fuel supplies: we have only enough oil left for a short period and coal supplies will hold out for only a limited time beyond then. Yet so long as each con-sumer is free to burn more, he hastens the day when there is none left for anyone. All of us are touched by this in-exorable logic: until we are prepared to forgo this 'free-dom', we are committed to our own destruction. Similarly, each motorist who takes a new car on the road, while en-joying full benefit to himself, immediately reduces the benefit to every other motorist. Before long every motorist is snarled up in traffic jams, and new roads can only be built at the expense of highly finite land resources and in pref-erence to other social needs out of a finite national budget. Again, as we shall see, each extra airborne passenger travels at the cost of the peace of mind of those under his flight path: each tourist contributes to the disappearance of the tranquillity or authenticity he seeks.

Most progress has been achieved in defiance of this logic. Almost all the efforts of technology have gone into pro-duction, virtually none into conserving resources or dealing with waste. To survive beyond tomorrow, man will have to adapt to the levels that our planet and the delicate balance of the biosphere will tolerate. 'What is required', says Paul Ehrlich, Professor of Biology at Stanford University, 'is no less than a revolution in human behaviour, one which em-bodies fundamental reforms in our economic and political institutions coupled with the wisest technological enter-prises, the necessary ingredient of population control and a new perception of man's place in nature.'

In Britain, the manifesto of revolutionary changes such as

17

those outlined above has now been published, its basic principles supported by well over a hundred scientists from a wide range of disciplines. Known as the *Blueprint for Survival* it coincided with the launching, early in 1972, of the Movement for Survival, the stated objective of which was to influence governments into taking measures most likely to lead to the stabilization and survival of society. The movement aims to achieve political status at the next election. The Blueprint's remedies are discussed in some detail in Chapter 13; they are so far-reaching, so contrary to conventional wisdom as to seem initially impossible. They are based on the premise that to survive, society must satisfy four main conditions: it should cause the least possible disruption to ecological processes; conserve materials and energy; hold population numbers steady and develop a social system in which people, unrestricted by the foregoing, enjoy life more.

Such changes will be unpopular at first. The transition period will take several decades if hardship is to be avoided, and may well prove to be this country's greatest challenge ever. To overcome apathy – the first requisite – may be the hardest battle of all. When Captain Cook sailed into Botany Bay, the aborigines, he records, who had never seen anything remotely like his ship, went about their business as if it were not there. Like these aborigines, in the face of impending, incomprehensible peril the majority today ignore it. They hope it will go away. For it is not only the premature extinction of the human species that threatens. In the polluted waters of Lake Erie a new mutant of carp has been reported that actually lives off the poisons in the water. The carp has, chillingly, adapted itself to a lower quality of life and – whether fact or legend – is nevertheless a graphic symbol of the danger now facing mankind. Like the half-blind mutant, he himself could adapt to a lower quality of life and yet survive.

What, the reader will ask, can *I* do about it? In a vast and complex society like ours, the individual has never felt more socially impotent and alienated. Yet in fact the first

18

step is a simple one: question what is happening in your district. Do you like the new motorway that towers over homes, the lorries scattering crowds in the high street, the long, long wait for the crawling bus? Are you growing used to the din of the low jets, from which the countryside no longer offers escape? Will you miss the village, bulldozed to extend an airfield? Can you remember when you used to catch fish from your river? Do you enjoy queuing with the crowds in the once-quiet seaside town, or the view of the tall, brash hotels lining the oily, trash-strewn beach? Is it all happening with your consent? No? Plenty of other people feel as you do. Seek them out, act in concert and the second step can be achieved.

This book is an attempt to help take the first two steps. It examines the implications of unharnessed growth and the spread of 'civilization'; it seeks to discover the point of no return in the many areas that threaten our way of life, to set out the possible alternatives for society, and to suggest some of the more constructive ways to avoid the crisis that moves closer every day.

2 Economic Perversion

Cars and aircraft have a magic which can hypnotize: they possess the capacity to attract funds for growth which other industries lack. Together with oil they typify the phenomenon which Sir Frank Fraser Darling described in the 1969 BBC Reith lectures: 'That 19th-century conception of inevitable and absolute progress is still believed,' he said, 'and it pushes us forward, rather than it leads us on to that which we truly desire. Technology is apt to condition us psychologically, so that man becomes its servant, no longer its creator and master . . . the supersonic aircraft *must* be produced simply because it can be.' This process of an ever-accelerating rate of growth in pursuit of obscured aims he christened the 'technological exponential'. In the modern industrial society the faith in progress which he portrayed is manifested in the ample funds for research, development, production and marketing which find their way into favoured industries. For, as Charles Tillinghast, chairman of Trans World Airlines said: 'What is technically and economically possible will be done.' The ultimate power which determines the allocation of such funds is vested with the super-large companies and governments. It is they who decide which industries shall benefit from technological research and development – much of it subsidized by the Government itself. And it is within the large companies that the marketing men possess their special power: to rouse people's latent needs so that in satisfying their ensuing desires more and more of the output of the favoured industries is consumed.

The oil, motor vehicle, aircraft and tourist industries

amply benefit from such collusion. Combining the advantages of large companies, government aid and marketing know-how, they have grown fat while basic needs of housing, health and education are ignored. They have benefited from the growing and convenient delusion that the principal aim of transport and travel is to make *movement* enjoyable, rather than life itself.

When there existed just the private sector, small groups of men fulfilled the community's basic needs, while government kept to the job of governing. Then the private sector divided: some groups stayed as small companies while others grew large, possessed with an inner dynamism that generated still more growth. Government began to change its role so that it should not be left out of the act and widened its scope, spreading to areas once the sacred domain of the private sector. It raised capital and began providing goods and services itself. Soon afterwards it started lending money to the large companies in the private sector and formed an alliance with them, so that it became their biggest single customer.

After the Second World War, the large companies began to attract in numbers men with talent and energy to form a decision-making upper stratum which Professor John Kenneth Galbraith aptly called 'the technostructure'. This group contained the diverse technical knowledge and experience which modern industrial technology demanded, and it quickly set about maximizing its success as an organization within each company, appropriating the power that had once resided with directors and shareholders. An interaction began between the technostructure and the company to which it belonged: while the company needed growth the requirements of technology were stability and power. New products and model changes were taking longer and longer to bring to fruition, and the amount of necessary capital investment was becoming alarming. So to minimize risk, the large company took steps to gain control over its suppliers and its markets of the future.

During the buoyant post-war years, growth, as measured in sales revenue, became the goal that superseded profits. Each member of the technostructure predictably identified himself with the growth goals of the company, and the technostructure adopted them for itself. All that remained was to ensure that the economy – its consumers in aggregate – felt the same way.

Consumers came in two sizes: 'giant government' and 'regular'. Government presented no problem: votes depended on jobs, and jobs on growth; moreover, it too had its technostructure – departments and ministries similarly bent on personal gain and group growth. Whichever party was in power, co-operation between the technostructures of industry and government came about smoothly.

The aid which government gives to large companies assumes many guises, some subtle, some unashamed. The State willingly underwrites the research and development for civil and military aircraft. Governments are major customers of the construction industry, buying roads, bridges, airports and large buildings. They are major customers of companies of all sizes which supply defence needs. By the use of economic regulators, the British Government controls the fortunes of whole industries – especially the car industry, which the Government knows is highly sensitive to hire purchase regulations and changes in purchase tax. When key industries are in difficulties, the Government, if it wishes, sees them through. BOAC, BEA, British Leyland, Cunard, Upper Clyde Shipbuilders, Cammell Laird, Yarrow, Harland and Wolff, and Govan Shipbuilders are some of the companies that have benefited to the tune of many millions of pounds in recent years.

Governments are committed to seeing that technological change of any kind enjoys high social prestige, and the State then inspires or sponsors appropriate technical and scientific innovation. When major companies follow suit, the burden on the Government is correspondingly lightened. With such a sophisticated relationship it is not surprising that governments and large companies speak the same language. The dividing line then becomes blurred. They share the same goals of growth and innovation. Car manufacturers, roadbuilders, planemakers, tourist industries and oil producers alike have thus all enjoyed unprecedented growth. Today up to one-fifth of Britain's Gross Domestic Product is involved directly and indirectly in moving goods and people from place to place. This proportion includes the industries making motor vehicles, railway stock, aircraft and ships, plus the cost of roads and airports and all dependent industries – engineering, fuel and so on.

The individual consumer has also played the role desired of him not only by buying and using the end products of industry but also by providing his labour as required. The nature of commerce and industry involves an unending movement of people and goods from one part of the world to another. By ship, train, lorry and plane, with all the regularity and monotony of peristalsis, the motion must go on. It would indeed be unfortunate for the system if individuals who make it work decided to free themselves from the Protestant ethic of compulsive labour – the concept that almost *any* work is noble, and inactivity somehow wrong. The time is perhaps nearer when workers will become disenchanted with the end products of their labour; planes they may never fly in, roads that replace homes, goods they can never possess – and begin to oppose the ample supply of capital from government and investors for planes, cars, roads and airports, which is denied to homes, schools and hospitals. The individual purchaser might even fall victim to the idea that a five-year-old car would be no reflection on his status and remain unmoved by the thrilling news that one detergent bleaches his sheets whiter than another. Man's appetites and curiosity have been to date only too conveniently susceptible to the alarums sounded by the companies' marketing men.

In an advanced society, purchasing is the expression of complicated emotional needs – no longer concerned with the basic necessities – food, shelter and clothing, but with an attempt to establish an identity and seek the kind of stimulation to reinforce it. Once the marketing men had grasped this, they were quick to attach psychological extras to the products they were selling. The desire for possessions could then be married with the craving for experience, and new products could be sold less as things, more as promises. 'Sell the sizzle, not the steak' was the genesis for this development in persuasion. It approached the summit of sophistication when car manufacturers put a surfeit of knobs and dials on dash boards to give drivers that James Bond feeling. So long as demands can be stimulated, the marketing men have done their job. The ventures that companies embark upon are determined by the ease with which desire for their products and experiences can be aroused. Neither they nor their marketeers are very concerned whether the ultimate mass market demand represents a beneficial way of life. As Professor Galbraith has said: more cigarettes cause more cancer, more automobiles cause more accidents, maiming and deaths, and more pre-emption of space for highways and parking, and more pollution of the air and the countryside. A high standard of living is simply an arrangement for avoiding muscular exertion, and increasing sensual pleasure and over-eating. He observes that whenever production goes up, people assume things are getting better.

The power to shape society, to determine the ideals to which mankind should aspire, has passed from the old authorities – statesmen, religious leaders, teachers, philosophers, poets, authors, artists and architects – to the faceless men of the technostructure. The result is an economy wedded to trivia, neglecting basic essentials. The economist, Edward Mishan, has observed that there is little evidence that social welfare improves with an increase in the index of economic growth. The phrase 'growth potential' is highly emotive, suggesting waste when it is not realized. It implies that the nation is a power house with everyone plugged in to generate 'industrial output'. The harmful effects of growth for its own sake do not stop there, however. The Royal Commission on Environmental Pollution

24

(1971) pointed out that 'the output of goods and services which gives rise to pollution tends to be pushed beyond the socially optimum point'. In other words, industry shows unconcern beyond the immediate benefits to itself and its customers, and output is pushed upwards to the point where the ill-effects of pollution exceed any possible benefits. Pollution costs are not borne by those who cause pollution nor even by those who buy what is produced. They are suffered by society as a whole, and especially by the poor, who are least able to protest or move to a better place. At no time in Britain's history has this sombre truth been brought home more poignantly than on that October day in 1966, when a man-made avalanche of wet slag engulfed the school, homes and children of the small Welsh coalmining town of Aberfan.

The Multinationals

Large companies, the marketing industry and the dependent mass media have been the prime movers in creating the kind of society in which we live. Britain has industrial and financial giants of her own, but the largest companies of all are the multinationals: the giant organizations whose activities span the world. Their sales are estimated to be worth 300 billion dollars a year, nearly two-thirds by American companies. Many of them – car manufacturers, plane makers and oil firms – are central to the mobility crisis. Certainly all of them, in their commitment to growth, generate excessive movement of people and goods, both directly and indirectly. And they are instrumental in the spread of global uniformity, for to maintain long production runs and justify heavy investment they must market their goods and services across national boundaries. They span the world, building their plants where it suits them, selling their standardized products wherever profitable. Their activities transcend governments, for they can switch imports and exports from base to base at will, and freely transfer huge sums from one country to another. Governments fear them, but woo them for their power to alleviate the problems of scarce capital and chronically depressed areas. They fear them because the important decisions are made on the top management board in the home base – usually the USA – and safely insulated from the people affected for good or ill by its decisions. The dominant aim of the multinational is to further its own interests, and these are independent of the interests of any government, whether its own or that of any of its subsidiaries. One such colossus is General Motors Incorporated of America. Its annual sales of over $25 billion are more than the net national income of all but some dozen nations. A company this size can control many of the prices of its raw materials and the selling prices of many of its products – aware that in a price war no one benefits; it can also control the design of products in its markets and since General Motors makes roughly half of America's cars, the designs it chooses become the fashion. General Motors is not the size it is for reasons of efficiency but simply because size enables it to plan with precision, control the market and reduce risks.

To counter shrinking home markets, more and more US companies are going international; the country's share of the international investment scene is now around 60 per cent. They are deeply entrenched in the United Kingdom. Between 1962 and 1968, overseas investment, apart from oil, insurance and banking, rose from £1.4 billion to £2.7 billion – two-thirds of it American. In 1969, the USA owned some 13 per cent of British industry and accounted for 16 per cent of British exports.

In 1969 the four biggest multinationals were General Motors (US), Standard Oil of New Jersey (US), Ford (US), and Royal Dutch/Shell (Holland/UK), with a combined gross turnover of over £24 billion. Such companies are nations outside nations. One factor links the top four, apart from size: they are all part of the mobility industry. Mobility is well represented in the big league. At least a fifth of the top hundred British and European companies are in it: eight in motor vehicles, seven in oil, three in tyres and two in ships and aircraft. To fulfil their growth objectives, these companies are forced to use the full weight of their technology, finance and influence to keep people and goods increasingly on the move. And since the products of one super-company look like another's, are priced like another's and *are* like another's, they succeed in imposing the Western way of life, principally American, on all people as the universally desirable goal, and local differences of culture, architecture and landscape are eventually swamped. They would reduce miraculous and infinite variety to the monotony of one globe-spanning Hilton. It is in the interests of the multinationals and other exporting companies within the over-developed countries to export the gospel of economic growth to the rest of the world. Lured by this tempting carrot, the governments and industrialists of the under-developed countries seek to catch up by investing in Western-style industry or selling their birthrights. The alien industrial philosophies which the developing countries embrace are capital-intensive, whereas their needs are labour-intensive; moreover, United Nations figures show that these countries now have to repay over a third of their hard currency income to the advanced nations as interest and amortization on past debts, and the proportion is expected to rise soon to half. Whatever they do the gap grows wider. In 1971 the United Nations Food and Agriculture Organization found that the world's 2.4 billion hungry poor were getting hungrier. On past growth rates it would take India over a century to reach the USA's present GNP per head; Nigeria would take over 300 years, and Indonesia 600 years. The plain truth is that the developing nations never will catch up. In 20 to 35 years a typical under-developed country will double its present population, unless checked. So in order merely to hold its present living standards it must *double* not only its production of food, but power, transport, roads, housing, doctors, teachers too. A daunting task for a rich country; an impossible dream for a poor one.

Long before the Third World could catch up, the Earth's

resources would be exhausted, pollution would have become intolerable, and the stocks of scarce, essential resources would be guarded by the strong elite nations. Even today, the USA with only six per cent of the world's population, consumes a third of the world's energy and a quarter of its minerals. It imports 80 per cent of its mineral requirements, mostly from under-developed countries. In 30 years the world's population will be 30 times that of the USA today. Not all the technology nor ingenuity of man can transform the dream of catching up into a reality.

3 Abrasive Oil

ONE mammoth industry has provided the power for the technological exponential and especially the unprecedented rise of transport and travel: oil. Once oil had been discovered, and in time found useful, more and more uses had to be found to keep up with the supply. It has been called the philosopher's stone of the twentieth century, and modern industrial states have become so dependent on it that without it they would no longer exist as such. Not surprisingly oil has become a prime concern of governments, colouring diplomacy and seeping into home and foreign policies. Wars have begun over oil, and they have been won because of it, or lost from a lack of it. The Second World War has been called 'The Petrol War', not only because the forces on both sides depended on it, but because so much of the fighting and bombing was to capture or destroy oil resources. Today, South East Asia has attracted multi-million-dollar investments in oil exploration by US, British and French companies. Some 5,000 Americans have requested an enquiry by Senator Fulbright's Committee on Foreign Relations into the activities of the economic lobby, sceptical of President Nixon's claim that the US was fighting in Indo-China on a matter of principle rather than for profit. Since an estimated profit of $5.8 billion from oil already flows to the US every year, it would not be surprising to find it taking steps in promising places to maintain or even increase the flow.

The government of any industrial state with a semblance of democracy knows that it relies on the oil industry, not only for economic growth, but for the contentment of its electorate on which its continuance largely depends. Even though it fears the industry for its power and the threat that such power poses, it must 'act friendly'. Oil companies are international organizations living in a nationalistic world, and they find themselves in turn threatened by governments which would take them over given the least opportunity.

No government dare put itself in the position of being without oil in an emergency, and so, as a safeguard, many governments have formed national oil companies – much to the annoyance of the American-dominated Oil Establishment. Besides the practical aspect, national pride is at stake, for no self-respecting country wants to be without its own oil industry – refineries and all. In this emotional, uneasy relationship, one factor remains stable: both industry and government want growth. So growth there is. Oil consumption has doubled in the past decade and, on present trends, promises to double again within the next one. The industry expects to sell more oil in the next 15 years than it has found in the last hundred. Since transport accounts for roughly a third of all the oil produced, highway policies, air travel subsidies, military expenditure – all government-inspired – help to encourage the oil industry's growth. In addition to these there is the Oil Depletion Allowance, an extension of the normal device by which companies can write off the cost of capital equipment against tax. The oil industry in the US has considered that the same principle should apply to its own capital costs, namely the rent which it pays on oil deposits. This, the Oil Depletion Allowance, has enabled rents to be partially offset against profits – and so led to the production of more oil for sale at lower prices.

Oil companies today are highly public relations conscious, ultra-sensitive to public reaction against the sting in their product's tail. Not only are oil's waste products the major cause of air pollution, but oil products themselves are giving the industry a bad name; for weedkillers, insecticides and detergents are all made from oil, and all have been the focus of environmental concern. Unfortunately the list does not end there: man-made fibres and plastic containers are spin-offs from the oil industry and both are defilers of seaside and countryside. The chemicals from which they are made are not usually bio-degradable, and so they resist the bacteria which cause natural decomposition of many other substances. But none of these nuisances cause more hostility to the oil industry and damage to its image than pollution of the world's oceans and beaches with waste oil. Thor Heyerdahl reported seeing visible oil pollution for 43 days out of 57 during his Atlantic voyage aboard the raft, Ra II. For Britain alone, the 1971 cost of dealing with the nuisance was over £530,000, a sixfold increase in only four years. Marketing men used to complain that oil was tough to advertise because it was used without being seen: now it is embarrassingly visible on most of the tourist beaches they helped to create. Oil is one of the most odious pollutants: to swimmers and sunworshippers from Margate to Majorca it is a reminder of the price they pay for cheap travel; to taxpayers it is a heavy expense; to birds and marine life it is slow extermination: to seamen it can mean death.

Oil reaches the sea in three ways: the cleaning or draining of tankers' ballast tanks at sea, fuel dumping by nontankers, and wrecks or collisions. Two-thirds of the Earth's surface are ocean, and when oil took over as the chief motive power for transport and industry, it obligingly absorbed the attendant spillage. In attempting to alert all concerned that the ocean might not always be so accommodating, the early environmentalists, predictably, met with little success. The first international conference on ocean pollution by oil was called by the USA in 1926 but little was achieved. In the early 1950s naturalists and scientists expressed renewed concern, and, after help from the United Nations, a treaty was agreed in 1954 which put in motion a series of restrictions on discharging oil at sea. But the restrictions were neither enforced by governments nor observed by sea captains and the shipping lines that employed them. In 1969 an assembly of the Intergovernmental Maritime Consultative Organization broke through the apathy barrier and adopted recommendations which would have reduced oil pollution drastically. However, by 1971, out of 30 member states, only six had accepted them, and when the assembly met again the problem was described as developing with 'alarming speed'. According to the Swiss oceanographer, Professor Piccard, nearly 10 million tons of oil products are now dumped in the ocean every year.

A modern tanker empties up to 200 tons of oil each time it cleans its tanks. The easiest and cheapest place to do so is at sea and certain zones have now been agreed where this may be done. Ocean traffic however is still not adequately covered by agreements – and oil tankers make up 40 per cent of such traffic. Discharging oil at sea therefore continues – one more example of 'technology on the cheap'.

Tank-cleaning is unspectacular, continuous and unheeded, but oil pollution from collisions at sea is rather more difficult to keep out of the news. On March 18th 1967, mankind woke to learn that, along with the Bomb, lung cancer and the Silent Spring, they now had to live with the daily peril of mass pollution by super tankers. On that day the 974-foot long supertanker, *Torrey Canyon*, bound for Milford Haven with a cargo of 117,000 tons of crude oil, struck the Seven Stones Rocks just east of the Isles of Scilly. She made history, not only because of the terrifying size of her cargo and the ensuing calamity, not merely because of the bizarre circumstances of the collision and subsequent drama, but because, almost overnight, she alerted the world to a new peril. This 'floating oil well' spilled its cargo into a tideway, which soon became a carrier of destruction, as the vast slick drifted from the Cornish beaches to the Channel Islands and the coast of Brittany with all the unpredictability of roulette – in agonizing slow motion. Wherever it landed, it killed mercilessly. Tens of thousands of seabirds died, despite tireless rescue work, and some rare species were reduced to near extinction; countless shellfish perished, and with them the minute forms of marine life on which the ocean's eco-system depends. The effects of the oil and the millions of gallons of detergents used to combat it were not only immediate, they were longlasting. Early estimates put the recovery time for marine life in the affected districts as a decade from D-day, but in March 1972 reports of a new oil slick near the wreck, and hundreds of dead and oil-soaked birds gave rise to fears that oil was escaping from it; if so recovery time would be even longer.

The immediate cause of the disaster was human fallibility. Only when the responsibility assumes the proportions of ferrying 117,000 tons of poison in an unwieldy, ill-designed ship of 118,000 tons dead-weight, through crowded ship-ping lanes to maintain a tight commercial schedule do the consequences of such fallibility lead to ecological disaster. It has been authoritatively estimated that the total cost to the British and French Governments, insurers and others ex-ceeded £10 million.

Before *Torrey Canyon*, the most serious oil spillage in British waters had been a mere 10,000 tons. Throughout 1966 there were 105 reports of ships either leaking oil or disposing of it in British coastal waters; in 89 reports the vessel was named. That year there were 46 convictions for illegally discharging oil into the sea, yet the average fine in each case was only about £100. In the three years pre-ceding the *Torrey Canyon* disaster there had been 329 incidents where tankers had collided or run aground. In 16 of these, the ships were total losses.

A committee, set up under Sir Solly Zuckerman after the *Torrey Canyon* accident, examined the current and pro-jected sea traffic in British coastal waters and came up with a disturbing prediction: with 300,000 ships using the Straits of Dover each year alone, there was 'a very real possibility that another incident involving a tanker of over 30,000 tons deadweight will occur in the next ten years or so around our coasts'.

Only since the last world war has ocean pollution by oil become a visible problem for Britain. Until then most of Britain's liquid fuel imports were as refined oil. Now crude oil is brought by tanker for refining on the spot – and the attendant pollution risk shows evidence of dramatic and disturbing growth. At the time of the *Torrey Canyon* disaster, on any day of the year the oceans were likely to be carrying some twenty-five million tons of oil products – most of this as crude oil bound for refineries. About a third of the world's shipping tonnage is devoted to carrying oil – a total of some 4,000 tankers.

Since the end of the war the world's tanker fleet has doubled in size and capacity every ten years, but *total* fleet size is not the only figure to show growth, for in the same period tankers have grown longer, wider and heavier, and the loads they carry have increased in proportion. During World War Two the common tanker deadweight was 16,000 tons. By the end of the war marine engineers were talking of an ultimate deadweight increase up to 24,000 tons. Technology, like the oil industry that it was harnessed to serve, was dedicated to growth. If bigger ships could be built . . . they would be. In 1968, the first of a series of Japanese tankers of 276,000 tons deadweight was launched. In 1971 two tankers each 477,000 tons deadweight were on order from Japan, and Shell were reported to be negotiating with a French shipbuilding group for five ships, each 500,000 tons. John Kirby, chairman of Shell Tankers (UK) has predicted that there will be several ships over 500,000 tons by the end of the decade, and possibly some of one million tons.

The oil companies surprised themselves with the huge savings that gigantic ships could make; with the closing of the Suez Canal a new page in the accounts books was opened. For a round trip from, say, Kuwait to Milford Haven, the cost of moving oil goes down as tonnage goes up. Naturally, as tankers grow larger, pollution risks increase: in the event of grounding or collision the quantity of poisonous crude oil likely to be released uncontrollably is correspondingly greater; and the ability of the master to avoid disaster is proportionately reduced.

While the *Torrey Canyon* oil was still pouring from its hull, Prime Minister Harold Wilson called on the United Nations Intergovernmental Maritime Consultative Organization (IMCO) to meet in extraordinary session with the express brief of considering how maritime law and international regulations could be changed to reduce the risk of repetition of such a disaster. IMCO put forward eight proposals to combat the new peril: traffic lanes at sea; certain areas to be off-limits to tankers; large tankers to carry more navigational aids; a speed limit for large ships near land; tankers to be stronger – possibly with double hulls; tankers to have protruding flaps or towed drogues for quicker stopping; ships to have adequate charts and sailing directions; and officers and crew to be better trained in the use of navigational aids, and the aids to be periodically tested.

People outside the shipping and oil world welcomed the proposals; those directly interested in keeping down oil transport costs were less enthusiastic. Some proposals, such as double hulls, were rejected outright; others, it was urged, would have either marginal effect or were already operative. The reaction closely resembled that of the car makers to safety and pollution proposals for their industry.

The depressing, overall conclusion to be drawn was that the proposals would not have prevented the loss of the *Torrey Canyon*. Similar disasters will happen more often. In 1970 the world's tanker fleet was 38 per cent of the world's total merchant fleet tonnage – a significant increase over the previous year. Tanker tonnage accounted for over half the increase in the world fleet during the year. IMCO has as its declared objective the complete elimination of wilful and intentional oil pollution by 1975, but unless improved technologies are vigorously applied and enforced, future disasters can be expected to have even more devastating effects on people and the species with which they coexist.

On a world scale ocean pollution is the oil industry's major ecological headache, but within Britain's boundaries the environment faces a different threat. The whole of Britain is now mapped out for systematic on-shore oil prospecting, with disastrous prospects for the farmlands, National Parks and other areas of natural beauty. If oil is found, it will be of relatively little value to the nation – merely easy money for the oil companies. Britain now uses over 110 million tons of oil a year. Oil is already produced on-shore: about 83,000 tons a year, equal to 0.07 of Britain's annual requirements. Even if drilling were successfully multiplied a hundred times, the yield would last barely a month at today's consumption rates – with unthinkable consequences for the countryside. But consumption is rising so fast, that its value would soon shrink to even less. The copious North Sea deposits were estimated in 1971 to yield 30 million tons a year, yet by the time the oil is piped ashore, Britain's annual demand for oil will have risen by roughly that amount, and we shall be back to square one. With this kind of arithmetic any interference with Britain's pitifully small scenic reserves is grave cause for concern.

Oil is the remains of teeming prehistoric life, trapped for millions of years as much as 13,000 feet deep. In such abundance and with such a past, it has been assumed to have a long future, but in 1971 a senior British Petroleum geologist, Harry Warman made some startling predictions. The oil industry had found 102 billion tons of oil and burned 31 billion. Using 2.4 billion tons a year, as we now do, there is enough to last till the year 2001. But each year we use more – about 7.5 per cent. One estimate says we shall use more oil in the seventies than in all the years preceding. If no more oil were found, it would all be gone by 1987. The industry reckons it must always have ten years' known supplies in reserve. If none had been found in the sixties we would be in trouble now. Harry Warman estimates that new finds are yielding only 2½ billion tons a year – hardly enough to keep pace with demand. To maintain that magic ten-year reserve, oilmen must find another 95 billion tons before 1990. And that is almost all they have found to date. In the 1990s they must find another 54 billion to keep going – equal to the whole of the North Sea field *every three months!*

By the year 2000 we shall be running short, and Britain will be competing with every other industrial nation for every drop she can get. The world will look back in anguish at the days when we squandered such an unexpectedly miraculous and finite resource by burning it in cars and in tourist-packed aircraft. What little is left will be saved for essential air travel and chemical manufacture – including possibly synthetic food. Looked at in the long history of mankind, the present industrial surge, now in its 150th year, may be seen as a short-lived phenomenon of doubtful merit, made possible only by the swift exploitation of finite fossil fuels, principally oil.

4 The Cost of the Car

A TREE has no need to be mobile, for it lives in its own food supply, but as life forms become more complex so the need for mobility increases. Primitive man had a food problem, for he was competing with swifter creatures than himself, but his brain came to his aid and in time he learned to tame and ride the horse. With the discovery of the wheel, man was able to move himself and his goods faster and easier, and since then the quest for mobility has continued apace. In 6000 BC the camel caravan could travel some eight miles an hour. In 1600 BC the chariot reached about twenty miles an hour, and not until the 1880s did steam locomotives better that record with speeds up to a hundred miles an hour. The first steam locomotives of 1825 reached only thirteen miles an hour and the first mail coaches in 1784 travelled a mere ten mph. In less than 60 years however the speed limit had quadrupled: by 1938 aircraft had achieved 400 mph; by the 1960s rocket planes had raised the limit tenfold to 4,000 mph and spacecraft were cruising at 18,000 mph. This is the speed dimension of the mobility explosion which displays all the characteristics of exponential growth. Most people are used to thinking of growth as a *linear* process – a constant increase through time: in exponential growth the increase occurs ever more rapidly through time – only the percentage of increase is constant, and so growth towards the end of any time period is far more rapid than at the beginning. Later in the book we shall study the effects of such growth as manifested by air travel; in this chapter we encounter the effects of road transport.

The car began life innocently enough, seemingly an invention full of benefit and promise, offering man instant independence and freedom from the shortcomings of public transport. Yet in its 85 years of existence the car has insidiously eaten its way into the fabric of society, growing ever more demanding as it remorsely consumes the vital strands and spreads its excreta. The enormity of the havoc is now being recognized, yet society is allowing itself to become ever more dependent on the car.

It kills and maims more people than a continuing medium-sized war. It pollutes the air and fills it with noise. Its highways consume land and buildings wholesale – not even scarce housing is spared. The highways scar the countryside; they dictate the shape of our cities, and that shape is unlovely and inhumane. Because the car is beyond the reach of many, and always will be, it robs them of means of contact with others, for the bus and train steadily disappear. The car requires neither its maker nor its owner to pay his fair share of the costs of the havoc it creates; its drivers enjoy motoring on the cheap at the expense of the taxpayer. The car costs more than society can afford, diverting valuable resources of funds and skill from more urgent and needy priorities. It is an inefficient, dangerous, ill-designed mechanical blunder, vulgar on its own, ugly *en masse*. But this is the price that all of us pay so that some of us may enjoy a private transport system.

Some have seen an alternative, however, and from the parents of child accident victims, from citizens with homes lost to road 'improvements', from those who cannot drive, from enlightened town planners and politicians, a chorus of criticism is swelling. Professor Colin Buchanan has said of the car: 'Apart from war, it is difficult to think of any previous activity of man that has wrought this . . . havoc.' And in his government-commissioned report he said: 'Given its head, the motor vehicle would wreck our towns within a decade.' From car designer Alec Issigonis, creator of the Mini, comes the warning that the motor car is ruining our civilization.

39

Predictably however the car industry views its products in a different light, and it campaigns vigorously for the right of every man and woman to drive their own cars. In 1968, Lord Stokes, the Chairman of the British Motor Corporation declared: 'The man and the woman in their cars in the street, quite evidently have concluded that, if they exist by breathing and eating, they live by moving . . . Our task is to provide the vehicles they require, and the services to keep those vehicles on the road – as simple as that . . . So without more ado, I suggest we get on with it.' He had an equally ecstatic protagonist in Edward Heath who as Conservative leader opened the 1966 Motor Show with an exhortation that we abandon ourselves to the car at any price: 'Some people', he said, 'would like to push us into a frame of mind in which it is considered anti-social to own a car; selfish to drive one; and positively sinful to take it into a built-up area. Of course traffic in towns creates a problem . . . my approach is not to restrict, to hamper or confine the motorist. Instead we must learn to *cope* with the motor car and care for the motorist.'

But from President Nixon's adviser on urban affairs, Daniel Moynihan, has come a contrary opinion: 'More than any other single factor, it is the automobile that has wrecked the 20th century American city, dissipating its strength, destroying its form, fragmenting its way of life.' He speaks from the country where, as we shall see, the havoc speaks for itself. In a vast country such as America, where land is abundant and the cities are new, the car's ravages are saddening to witness, but they have taken away relatively little of irreplaceable value as yet. The culture that was emerging at such alarming speed was hell-bent for some such machine and the car filled the need. But in a country like Britain – tiny, overcrowded, beautiful in an intimate way, rich in history and tradition, the same machine creates a holocaust. The countryside of Britain is a man-made work of inspiration – a painstaking blend of practical farming and aesthetic beauty. The cities, towns and villages even until recently retained much of their original streets, squares and parks – the largely unplanned, eminently workable arrangement of architectures that offered surprises round corners and displayed infinite variety of scale, texture, light and shade. One place was recognizably different from another. The citizens had a strong sense of identity. All this was irreplaceable, part of everything that was Britain and a magnet for tourists from America and elsewhere. Yet much of this asset is now disappearing. Using the fatal logic of the 'tragedy of the commons', each would-be car owner has set about improving his lot at the expense of the rest. The car – aided by the lorry – has proved to be a skilful rapist; the nation has accepted the inevitability of the experience, and has apathetically lain back and tried to enjoy it.

The statistics of the experience make awesome reading. At the turn of the century there were fewer than 8,000 cars on Britain's roads; by 1925 there were over half a million; by 1960 over five million, and in 1971 over 12 million. By 1980 the Road Research Laboratory predicts over 19 million. Between 1965 and 1969, traffic increased more than 20 per cent. In 1970 just on ten per cent of our total expenditure went on road transport, a two per cent rise within a decade. A major factor has been the jump in the number of company cars, now estimated to account for *nearly half* the spending on new cars, now rocketing as a result of tax relief granted in 1971.

The growth in goods vehicles has also been spectacular – in 1971 they exceeded 1.5 million. Britain's roads are officially predicted to carry over 23 million vehicles of all types by 1980, but since every official forecast to date has been outstripped in practice, all estimates are suspect. In America there are over 400 cars for every 1,000 people and the proportion is rising. The British figure is still under half that, but with more of an untapped market ahead, the gap may be expected to close. This country has more vehicles for every mile of road than any other major industrial country. If vehicle numbers and road building trends continued to the end of the century as they have over the past decade, there would be over 140 vehicles for every mile of road.

Britain already has 2¼ miles of road for every square mile of land, and new roads are being built at the rate of 1,200 miles a year. By the end of 1972 the country will be spanned by 1,000 miles of motorways and nearly as much in dual cariageway trunk roads. The Department of the Environment [*sic*] aims for 2,000 miles of motorways and 1,500 miles of trunk roads by 1980 at a cost of about £2.3 billion. Each mile of motorway consumes some forty acres of land. Yet England already has 910 people to the square mile – four times as many as China, 17 times as many as the USA. And every three or four years there are a million more – every year the equivalent of a city the size of Plymouth.

Such statistics for an overcrowded island might conceivably be justified if the end result were a transport system of superlative efficiency. But, as we shall see, road transport is a disastrous chronicle of death, destruction, congestion and misplaced effort.

Motorists, freight hauliers and their representative bodies complain repeatedly of high taxes. The cost of running a private car, now around £10 a week, they say is excessive. In fact they are getting their motoring on the cheap. Their contribution in fuel and vehicle taxes – around £1.8 billion a year – seems high, until the nuisances they create are totted up. Then it can be seen that, contrary to general belief, it is more than likely the taxpayer, whether car owner, road user or not, who is subsidizing the motorist. Consider the principal items:

Police: traffic and motoring offences account for around two-thirds of all indictable crimes. One-third of all police costs are estimated to be incurred over traffic, that is around £95 million a year. In provincial cities, police spend a quarter of their time on traffic duty. Throughout the country traffic duty is mainly responsible for the non-availability of scarce police resources for other work, thereby imposing an incalculable cost on the community in terms of crimes which might have been prevented and in crimes committed and unsolved.

Accidents: average cost per accident on the open road put at £1,600. Total cost of accidents estimated at £320 million. Over 400,000 vehicles annually involved in personal injury accidents. Some 13,000 hospital beds occupied by road accident cases at any one time – enough to fill 26 large hospitals. Nearly all medical costs paid by National Health Service.

Legal: since a high proportion of non-motorists are involved in accidents, legal costs are borne by the community. The burden of accidents, traffic and safety regulations now threatens to overload the entire legal system, imposing additional costs on all as a result. Motoring offences now number over 1.3 million a year.

Roads: construction costs paid by taxpayers, motorists and others amount to £550 million a year for main roads alone. The community also pays loss of home compensation to those who are displaced. Maintenance of roads paid by ratepayers, whether motorists or not, totals over £250 million a year.

Public transport: the run-down caused by cars (see Chapter 7) has resulted in the need for subsidies running at some £115 million a year, besides the extra cost to the community through delays and non-availability.

Noise: ten million people are affected by 'undesirably high' traffic noise according to the Road Research laboratory and this reduces property values at the community's expense. The Ministry of Transport has estimated the cost of traffic noise to the nation as between £30 and £40 million a year. (See pp 44-7)

Exhaust pollution: here the Ministry's estimate is £80 to £90 million a year. The total bill may be even higher when health, laundry, other cleansing costs and damage to buildings are included. (See pp 47-50)

Motor vehicle manufacturers and their suppliers account

43

for some six per cent of the Gross Domestic Product, but this is only a fraction of the total effort devoted to road transport, for it excludes all the items listed above plus the petrol and lubricating oil business, garages and service stations, accessories, tyres and batteries, marketing and sales effort, street furniture (traffic lights, signs and meters), traffic wardens, insurance and civil servants. If all these are included, road transport then accounts for no less than ten per cent of the Gross Domestic Product. It has been estimated that the industry directly and indirectly employs 11 per cent of the working population. The true social benefit of cost and effort on such a scale deserves close examination. Traffic is not only dangerous, smelly and hungry for space; as anyone living within a short distance of a main road will agree, it is disagreeably noisy, and buildings nearby tremble from the effects of vibration. Every ten years the noise in Britain's cities multiplies threefold, and traffic is the worst offender. Traffic noise at the levels experienced so far is not physically damaging; it does not bring on deafness, but it does make life more difficult and less enjoyable. Road traffic is unquestionably the most important individual sound heard by and bothering people when at home and when outdoors according to a recent Government Social Survey in London. The noise irritated 36 per cent of people at home and 20 per cent outdoors. According to the Road Research Laboratory, between 19 and 46 per cent of Britain's urban population of 45 million are subjected to intensities of traffic noise levels which are above the level considered desirable in residential districts. They predict a 50 per cent increase within ten years in the numbers of those who suffer noise.

But home and garden are not the only places where people suffer. In summer, countless office workers must choose between hot and quiet behind closed windows, or cool with open windows and the maddening roar of traffic. By permitting lorries to be heavier, by building more highways and by encouraging car output, the Government bears full responsibility for this situation. Lorries are among the chief offenders: not only have their numbers increased fourfold in eight years, but the maximum payload they may carry has been raised and when Britain enters the EEC, the Government can be expected to raise this yet again.

After years of wrangling, the first regulations on traffic noise finally became law in 1968. The maximum permitted noise levels were fixed at 89 decibels for lorries and 84 for cars. To most people decibels are about as familiar as dumb-bells; however some idea of their meaning can be gauged by the fact that heavy lorries are only just able to meet the specifications. A year after the regulations came into force the Minister of Transport admitted that the limits had been set too high 'We had to be realistic,' he said: 'It was no good setting limits that operators and manufacturers could not meet without putting an intolerable burden on vehicle users.' In 1971 he announced new measures: from April 1974 new buses and lorries would be limited to 86 decibels, cars to 80 decibels.

Despite these measures, years after the 1968 act, countless thousands of residents still suffer – except, that is, where they have adapted to a lower quality of life. The nuisance persists not only because the limits were set too high, but because they are rarely enforced. The police have found ample excuses; motorists' associations have predictably re-fused to co-operate; car makers and the haulage industry are delighted at the apathy.

But elimination of the worst offenders would not reduce noise sufficiently near main roads and motorways to make life fully enjoyable for near-by residents. At present the law covers only specific nuisances and it can neither prevent general noise levels from increasing nor can it reduce them. In 1971 the Association of Public Health Inspectors de-clared that Local Authorities should have power to declare 'Noise Control Areas' in the same way that they designate smoke control areas. However the Greater London Council has been advised that if it were made to buy a strip on either side of its motorways wide enough to reduce traffic

noise in homes by 30 decibels, the rehousing need would be more than doubled.

Control of the nuisance at source is the obvious starting point, but although the car industry spends lavishly on performance and styling, it is niggardly on reducing noise: silence *inside* is a selling point – consideration to the community is not! Yet the industry could be compelled to act if the public insisted. Noise could be cut and some engine power would go with it.

In any developments, whether widening roads, building new roads, enlarging airports or building new ones, a number of people are sure to suffer from the resulting increase in noise. Stephen Plowden, of Metra Consulting Group Ltd, has worked out a way of costing noise, so that the nuisance it creates can be set alongside the more tangible benefits of any developments. The study on which his findings are based were part of work done for the Roskill Commission on siting London's Third Airport. The findings, however, can be applied equally well to determine the cost of traffic noise. The study sought to establish how much money a person would have to be given, to compensate for the imposition of a noise nuisance.

A person affected has basically two choices: he can stay and endure the din, or he can move. In the study people were interviewed and, with special research techniques, asked to imagine they lived very close to a motorway with no danger, but with heavy traffic passing day and night. The study found that 58 per cent of owner-occupiers interviewed would move if adequately compensated. Some would need an average of over £2,000 minimum compensation while others were so reluctant to move that no compensation would suffice. If they were forced to accept dislocation costs limited to half the value of their property, then, they *would* move, but their price would be more than £4,000. Compensation in each case included all moving and repurchase costs, and took into account the loss in value of their present property. The remaining 42 per cent decided they would rather stay on and suffer the noise than endure the dislocation of moving. However they would need an average minimum compensation of nearly £700 each to do so.

These findings are significant. As Stephen Plowden has written: '. . . the decision may not be only where to build a motorway, but whether to build it at all, or rely more heavily on public transport instead.' At present, he said, what tends to happen is that the important decisions whether or not to go ahead with an investment are taken without much regard to environmental considerations. Yet they must be given their proper weight when important decisions are taken. It will quickly become apparent that, if the costs shown in the study were applied to motorway plans, instead of the current minimal compensation costs for people whose homes are to be demolished, the total costs would soar so high that most urban motorways would be ruled out of court – on noise considerations alone, irrespective of any others.

Scientists at the Road Research Laboratory have also conducted tests to learn the price people would put on different levels of noise. If this price were included in the cost of motorway construction and added to prices similarly obtained from tests on fumes and visual intrusion, some urban motorways could cost 50 per cent more. Furthermore, at the end of 1971 four firms of top consultants delivered a report to the Department of the Environment. It had been commissioned by the previous Government and it had taken 18 months to complete. The report reached a shattering conclusion: if urban motorways were built to the high standard necessary, and if the true costs of loss of amenity were included, their costs would more than double. If the Department were to accept the report few, if any, new urban motorways would be built.

All the flowers in the centre of Brighton, Sussex, were killed by traffic fumes during 1971 and the city's parks department had to consider ending its famous floral displays in busy traffic areas. In the same year, tests on a random sample of cars in London revealed that almost five out of six were emitting polluting exhaust fumes at a strength higher than would be allowed in Europe or the US. Flowers today people tomorrow . . . Each year in Britain the air has become more and more fouled with car and lorry fumes and, as poisons build up in soil and body tissues, a danger threshold may soon be reached.

The two chief poisons emitted by the exhausts of motor vehicles are carbon monoxide and lead. Carbon monoxide can affect hearing even at low concentrations of 50 parts per million. At higher levels simple problems become hard to solve, and at still higher levels eyesight is affected and muscular performance deteriorates. People with heart disease or emphysema may be particularly susceptible to low exposures. In industry the maximum tolerance in an eight-hour day is 50 parts of carbon monoxide in a million parts of air. At Oxford Circus in London the Air Pollution Research Unit has measured 360 parts to the million.

In New York, it is estimated that 98 per cent of the 2.5 million tons of carbon monoxide released in the city come from cars. Pedestrians in a busy street can be subjected to 50 parts per million – the level at which toxic effects can be detected. In Los Angeles there were on average 11 more deaths a day when carbon monoxide was at its peak compared with its trough.

Lead is now airborne around the world, virtually all of it from motor vehicle exhausts. The US discharges some quarter of a million tons into the atmosphere each year, Britain about 10,000 tons. As we breathe, so we build up lead in our bodies. Lead is a dangerous poison that respects no frontiers. Research has shown that the amount deposited on the Greenland icecap has risen rapidly in recent years; 300 per cent between 1940 and 1965. According to Professor Piccard 200,000 tons of lead enter the oceans every year and, with oil and other pollutants, are killing the plankton on which the marine life chain depends.

In 1971 the British Government ordered tests to be made on dust and dirt in the streets where children play, after receiving German reports that dust contained harmful exhaust emission contents. Soon after this action, scientists at the Department for the Environment stated they would examine the possibility that an increase in mental abnormality in young children might be due to poisoning by exhaust fumes. The projected study followed a startling report by Derek Bryce-Smith, Professor of Organic Chemistry at Reading University, that a five-year investigation had shown that no other poison had built up so rapidly in man as lead. 'People living in cities may absorb half their daily dose just by breathing,' he stated. In the past three years there had been an alarming increase in the number of children under ten suffering mental disturbance. His observations were supported by doctors in Switzerland who had noted an increase in depression, fatigue and headaches in people exposed to exhaust fumes. When they were treated for lead poisoning, 85 per cent recovered.

The human body has become accustomed to absorbing lead from food and water, but the extra dose from air may be taking the total input above the level of tolerance. When Bryan Silcock, Science Correspondent of the *Sunday Times*, studied the problem, he reported that the average amount of lead in the blood of city dwellers in developed countries such as Britain was already between a quarter and a third of the level at which serious effects of lead poisoning may start to appear – including irreversible brain damage. If this is so, it is not surprising that Professor Bryce-Smith has written: 'To my best knowledge no other toxic chemical pollutant has accumulated in man to average levels so close to the threshold for overt clinical poisoning.'

In 1971 the US Congress finally yielded to public pressure and passed a bill requiring that car manufacturers reduce poisonous exhaust emissions by 90 per cent by the year 1975. Henry Ford 2nd expressed the view of most of Detroit when he declared they had been set 'an impossible task', but later the company was reported to have achieved a breakthrough. As a result of the measures it was predicted that American motorists would pay an extra $3 billion dollars a year for petrol, while performance would fall and car costs would rise. In Britain the Government adopted a 'wait and see' policy pending further research, and was expected to announce its own legislation during 1972. By then major European countries had substantially reduced the lead content in their petrol and Britain was expected to follow suit.

Although lead and carbon monoxide are the principal exhaust poisons, others also threaten health, especially when added to those emitted by industrial and domestic pollutants. At the end of 1971, Dr Sanchez Murias, a leading Spanish cancer specialist, stated his conviction that atmospheric contamination in large cities was almost as significant a cause of lung cancer as cigarette smoking. He said that the Spanish Government was studying proposals to set legal limits to pollution from motor vehicles and other sources.

Liquefied petroleum gas is a satisfactory alternative to petrol and is non-polluting. However, its use in Britain was discouraged in July 1971 when the Government imposed a tax on its use for motor vehicles equal to that on petrol. This followed a statement by Peter Walker, Secretary of State for the Environment: 'We are waging war on pollution on all fronts.'!

5 Our Daily Dead

ABOUT every six minutes a serious road accident occurs somewhere in Britain; each day more than 20 people are killed and 1,000 injured – a third of them seriously. Beside these statistics the seriousness of noise, vibration and exhaust pollution seem insignificant. Yet people have been anaesthetized by statistics and safety propaganda so that they have become a part of life, accepted along with bad weather as inevitable. So to accept the unacceptable they must tell themselves that accidents only happen to *other* people – until the statistics catch up with them, as one day they must. For if trends continue, every child alive today has an even chance of becoming a road casualty during his lifetime. With luck he may be patched up quickly without ill effect. With less luck he may be physically unharmed, but carry with him the mental scar of another's death. He may have lain alone by the roadside, in the dark in agony before he was found. Or lie for the rest of his life, along with hundreds of others, neither quite alive nor yet quite dead.

This is the heaviest price paid for the benefits of road transport; in human terms far more terrible than sterile country or polluted air. In highly motorized countries, road accidents are the commonest cause of death in young people, and the most vulnerable of all are young men aged 16 to 25. The annual toll in Britain is over 350,000 casualties: over 7,500 killed and nearly 91,000 seriously injured. In the US the annual toll is 54,000 killed and four million injured. In the Western world it has been estimated that there are 130,000 killed and 1.7 million seriously injured on the roads each year: equivalent to the number killed in a medium

51

sized war. Britain alone has suffered over seven million road casualties since the last war, 300,000 of them deaths.

If the human species survives, one day its historians will study our civilization and marvel that its people tolerated the river of death that flows past its doors. They may not understand that we only accept cars and lorries because we have grown up with them, so that we notice them less and less and forget what life was like without them: adaptation to a lower quality of life.

Some observers have likened the traffic stream to a high tension wire, stretched along the edge of every pavement and charged with a lethal high voltage. In such a situation few parents would let their children run on an errand with a mere routine warning 'Mind how you cross the wire'. Yet not only do we wait to be picked off, one by one, in road accidents, but those who survive remain passive with traditional British stoicism. Not every country is so acquiescent: in Uganda during 1970 and 1971, 16 car drivers were beaten to death by enraged crowds after being involved in road accidents. In Israel the parents of child road accident victims have formed an association of protest and mutual help. In Britain there is little hope of winning votes to budge Government indifference except by organizing citizen action, for accident victims remain silent: either inarticulate or dead.

Compared with road accidents, the number of people killed annually through natural catastrophes is insignificant; yet road deaths receive scant mention by comparison. The murder rate is about one a day – high enough for concern, and each one gets a headline. Yet with a death rate 20 times as high, most road accidents are ignored. When the Hindenburg zeppelin caught fire in 1937 and 36 people died, the accident virtually put paid to airships as a form of commercial transport; yet with 40 people killed in Britain every other day, the car continues unchecked.

Why? It may be because horror fascinates rather than deters. Or it may be because, in the lives of most drivers a serious accident is still a rare event – something which only happens to others – and they continue to drive recklessly.

52

Because the inside of a modern car is so isolated, so much like a room, with its low, soft seats, carpets and radio, drivers are easily lulled into false security. The crushingly powerful dynamic forces that smash bone and tear flesh have no place in this cosy, family place. Yet they can be only a second away.

Two hundred and fifty vehicles lulled their drivers into this kind of security on just three days of multiple crashes on motorways in the 1971-72 autumn and spring peak fog weeks. On the first day, 66 vehicles piled up on the M6 motorway in Cheshire; autumn fog patches were unmistakable, fog warning lights were flashing, but ten people died and dozens were injured. A few days later, 70 vehicles repeated the horror on the M1 in Bedfordshire; this time seven died and 45 were injured. March 16th 1972 was a day of multiple crashes throughout Britain. In bright morning sunshine, 115 vehicles entered rolling fog banks on the M1 in Bedfordshire and Buckinghamshire; nine people died and 51 were injured. On each day most of those who died were incarcerated. Seat belts would have saved many of the dead and injured, but on motorways, less than half the drivers bother to wear them, and in city and suburban driving the proportion falls to one in ten. Surveys have shown that, despite the proven life-saving value of seat belts, the vast majority of motorists oppose any move to make the wearing of them compulsory. But seat belt apathy is not new: the Government began talks with the Society of Motor Manufacturers and Traders on compulsory anchorage points as long ago as 1961, yet it was not until 1969 that they were made a legal requirement for post-1964 cars.

Inertia grips official attitudes and actions. In a 1971 Road Research Laboratory survey, replies to 2,000 questionnaires showed that a large proportion of primary and secondary schools had no planned programme for teaching road safety and very little time was spent on it. The survey revealed moreover that only a third of the primary schools surveyed had safety barriers outside their entrances, even though 13 per cent of them opened onto roads with a 70 mph limit.

It is known that about 15 per cent of all victims with head injuries die because of impaired breathing in the first half hour after injury, yet because on-the-spot accident services are so inefficient, lives are being lost or permanent brain damage incurred by many who survive. The BMA has deplored the unnecessary suffering of the motorist involved in a serious accident. Since ambulance men can give only limited aid, the BMA called for a national accident service to fill the gap, but the response was nil.

Apathy, unfortunately, has a commercial value. Scares on road casualties are bad for business: they can deter would-be car purchasers and they lead to government action which forces manufacturers to make cars safer, initially at their own expense. There is therefore a strong vested interest in keeping the temperature low and minimizing the problem. This is not to say that there is any evidence of a sinister lobby, but merely a lack of initiative to act, which works to the benefit of business and the detriment of the public.

The AA and the RAC have not exactly taken the initiative either. They opposed increased penalties for motoring offences, the 'totting up' of endorsements, breathalyzer tests, compulsory testing of vehicles, raising the minimum age for motor cyclists, speed limits and legal 'teeth' to the Highway Code: all measures designed to reduce hazards and save lives. For instance, after the horrifying 1971 M1 pile-up, the Director-General of the AA, Mr A. C. Durie, suggested in a letter to *The Times* that in dense fog motorway traffic could move at 40 mph in safety!

The politician's traditional solution to the grisly problem is to pretend it does not exist unless pressed, then make high-sounding speeches castigating motorists and promising action, then vote a few more million for road improvements and a few thousand for safety campaigns and sit back with a sigh of relief. The radical legislation to make cars safer has been conspicuously absent. This pleases the growth pundits, the car manufacturers and road makers, but it does little to save lives. Whenever such a programme is announced, car manufacturers and motorists breathe again. They have escaped once more from paying for the measures that should be taken and, along with the rest of the community, they can feel reassured that 'something is being done'. Once again each individual can return to his usual state of inactivity, positive that the statistics he reads will still refer to people he does not know, and can quickly put them out of his mind.

There are three causes of accidents: people, vehicles and roads. Each is capable of improvement, but the very nature of road transport guarantees that there always will be accidents. To see how people cause them, let us first take a look at the different kinds of drivers and their motivations.

At the Road Research Laboratory, Psychiatrist Michael a'Brook has identified three main types of bad drivers. Least lethal, possibly, are those he terms 'injudicious'. Usually they are safe, but at times they lose concentration, misjudge things and take hair-raising chances. They are most dangerous when overtaking, which is unfortunate, because they enjoy doing this and hate being overtaken. Their passengers must get used to plenty of near-misses.

The second type is not quite aware enough to be safe. He tends to look fixedly ahead, and little things like crossroads escape his notice. He is unpredictable and impatient, with a tendency to drive too close to the car in front.

The third type also lacks the total awareness essential to avoid accidents, but lacks the second type's compulsive activity. He is overtaken on average five times more often than he overtakes and his specialities are right-turn and road junction accidents.

Any person may have skill and fitness, yet through personality defects turn into a bad risk. Worst of all is the person unduly sensitive to criticism, possibly inadequate, with a desperate need to prove himself. Highly competitive people would do best to travel by bus. Brains are a help in driving: it is a task so complex that it is barely within the human brain's capacity.

55

In the complex matrix of accident cause and effect, aggression emerges as an important factor. Professor A. F. Whitlock, psychiatrist and author, has studied this aspect and suggested that drivers look on their cars as pieces of movable real estate and defend them as such. Once in his car, surrounded by family possessions, a driver feels he must stand up for his rights, and in traffic he considers the road space as his hinterland, to be defended if a rival enters it, as when cutting in. Professor Whitlock has observed that in countries where the rate of such social violence as murder, suicide, rape and robbery is high, the rate of death on the road is also high, and the reverse also holds true. Thus he sees road deaths as an index of the amount of aggression in a society. He writes: 'In a society which sets a high value on the ownership of motor vehicles, it seems all too probable that those who have the greatest difficulty in controlling their aggressive propensities will be those most likely to manifest these tendencies through the driving of automobiles.'

In one British study 23 per cent of people convicted of serious traffic offences had also been convicted for other offences. Aggressive psychopathy is often a feature of people convicted of violent crimes, yet there is no ruling to withhold a driving licence from a psychopath. In another study, Meyer H. Parry, a psychologist at the University of Strathclyde, found that, in interviews with 382 drivers, no fewer than 27 admitted to having deliberately driven at another car, 45 had tried to edge another car off the road, and 32 had been involved in fights. He found that aggressiveness and anxiety were usually manifested together, and drivers with these personality traits had more than their fair share of accidents. A young bank clerk with strong feelings about the misuse of atomic energy and the way young people behaved, repeatedly used the North Circular Road like a race track and joked about knocking down a cyclist. A shipping clerk systematically rammed a car that parked irritatingly in front of him. A 20-year-old girl clerk raced a motorist who tried to overtake her, lost control when he succeeded, and woke up in hospital. In a society where the individual feels alienated and frustrated, the road provides a ready outlet for his feelings. In West Germany, which has one of the highest traffic fatality rates in Europe, tension on the roads has reached a pitch where animosity is leading to widespread violence. In April, 1972, one motorist shot and killed another only a few months after a motorist stabbed to death a pedestrian who annoyed him. Concerned by such incidents, the Munich Police Commissioner has said: 'Aggressions formerly released in wars are now being let loose on the road.'

Speeding offers an opportunity for release, and soon becomes a habit: to drive right to the limit of perceived safety can become the one totally absorbing occupation of each and every journey. To dart from lane to lane, to overtake, to corner at speed – all these bring to the driver the excitement and danger of the ancient hunt. When a motorist states how long it takes to get somewhere, he invariably quotes a time based on the highest speeds he can achieve.

In any motorized country, flouting the rules becomes a national pastime. Compared with others, motorists convicted of careless driving are found to use their mirrors less, give fewer signals, overtake dangerously and drive faster. In one study, over half the motorists interviewed admitted they did not always observe traffic laws. Most drivers simply do not understand what many of the standard road signs mean, and even experienced lorry drivers have been found to be ignorant of vital braking distances: in one recent survey only 11 per cent gave correct answers.

Drinking-and-driving have always been a problem: the Romans passed laws to try to reduce collisions between drunken charioteers. Breath tests have reduced accidents due to drink, but blood tests on victims in hospitals still show it as a prime cause. In the US over half the road fatalities are related to drinking-and-driving. So long as the car is identified as a piece of private territory, it seems that drink restrictions will be flouted: 'If I can drink as much as I like at home, I'll do so in my car.'

In studying accident causes and effects, one begins to encounter a chilling conclusion that road accidents are inevitable – an inescapable adjunct to the private road transport system. Effort can be made with training and propaganda, but, as with all education, little progress can be made to improve drivers unless they have the right home environment. At the Highway Safety Research Institute of the University of Michigan, research among 8,000 people showed that behaviour in traffic by younger drivers was influenced more strongly by the family – the father especially—than by driver education or the law. If parents take risks, speed, break regulations and boast about doing so, kids grow up to do the same. But this is not all, for there exists the deadly 'threshold effect': people can in time perhaps be educated, vehicles made safer for those inside and out, roads can be put in order, but there still remains one major loophole; improvements to vehicles and roads, far from reducing accidents, may even *increase* them. When road conditions are better, motorists drive faster so that the 'perceived risk level' stays constant, and when cars are made safer, motorists drive faster still, euphoric with their new-found protection. The combined effect is to raise casualty rates to 'normal' again – or worse. In other words, motorists drive up to a threshold, taking risks just short of creating the conditions which, in their view will cause an accident.

The standardized, industrial society fosters the use of the road as an outlet for the frustration and aggression it creates, and in the growing 'motor sport' industry it has come up with the convenient industrial answer: uninhibited worship of the Mobility God. Motor racing, hill climbing and rallying are all now in the web of big business, for as part of their publicity budget, car manufacturers and others invest millions in direct grants and promotion campaigns. Every year 1½ million people attend Britain's circuits, and motor sport has become second only to Association Football in popularity: over 13 million watch it on television.

In an in-depth interview, one enthusiast, a middle-aged ex-fighter pilot, revealed with candour just what the sport meant to him:

'There are two kinds of motoring,' he said: 'Getting from A to B or using the car as an expression of your personality. As a slightly irritable, aggressive person, I find the car as a mode of transport extremely irritating, because I have to obey all sorts of ridiculous rules. Which is why I also use it in competition – hill climbs, rallies and circuit racing. Circuits vary, but they all share one thing – you can let yourself go as hard as you like – it's a bit like being with a woman. If you make a mistake early in the race, and it doesn't happen to kill you, you stand some chance of catching up, so you need more skill than courage. There's an element of danger, of course; it's part of the point. The other is to win. I like winning. I don't like coming second, I'd sooner come seventeenth. I enjoy rallies because they employ two of my skills. One is actually driving motor cars, which I like doing, and driving them bloody fast; the other is that you can win a rally if you read the regulations carefully . . . get the checkpoints right and make no navigational errors. You're using all the driving skills you have and all the head you have. The car is an extension of myself. It is part of me. My favourite pulls over 210 – you're strapped in completely. If there's a crosswind you have to drive like hell to keep the car on the straight at all. Driving is a method of frustration release for many people, including me. But it's more than that. The motor car is "me plus". I can go faster in a car than I can go on my bloody feet, for chrissake! When the other bloke pulls next to you, what I do – and I know it's dangerous – is just move over, and he can have his accident if he likes. There are some nice, polite, good, kind drivers, who move over and let the other fellow through: I will move in and he can bloody well run up my arse as far as I'm concerned. I have this thing about a job, or a woman or cars – or whatever it is: if it isn't any fun, don't do it. The whole thing about driving is it's bloody nearly all fun – no boring patches. If

you relax for one instant one of two things will happen:
either you will get dead which is not required; or you will
be passed by somebody else who is concentrating harder
than you are, which is also not required. The aim of the
game is somehow to finish first. Who remembers who came
second?'

Pedestrians, as we shall see later, constitute a neglected
majority, and in no area is this neglect more apparent than
the prevention of accidents. Each year in Britain some
3,000 pedestrians are killed and 82,000 injured, and the toll
is rising. Pedestrians now account for nearly 30 per cent of
the total number of fatal and serious casualties; in London
half the people killed on the roads each year are pedestrians.
Those least able to look after themselves fare worst: 40 per
cent of the fatal and serious casualties are children and
another 25 per cent are people over sixty. Over half the
children die crossing the road, and in London 40 per cent
of them are knocked down in the street where they live.
Child casualties are rising: between 1959 and 1969, fatal
and serious casualty rates for child pedestrians aged five to
nine rose 34 per cent; for those between 10 and 14 they
rose a staggering 103 per cent. On present trends one child
in 50 is doomed to be killed by a motor vehicle. Those between the ages of three and ten are the most likely accident
victims.

In Stockholm, Professor Stina Sandels, of the Institute for
Child Development Research, has studied the vulnerability
of children, and she is emphatic: children under ten should
not be let out on the streets alone. Children see, but do not
comprehend as adults do; they are too small to see over
things and are more interested in what is near the ground;
they cannot see or read traffic signs, and the traffic rules
are too hard for them. In our machine-oriented society the
price of innocence is death.

In narrow streets, typical of many towns, the pedestrian
of any age faces increasing hazards, even in his rightful
place on the pavement. He risks being crushed by lorries of

disproportionate size and length – now increased to a permitted length of over 48 feet. If he is no longer safe on his own pavement he is in mortal danger whenever he steps off it. Zebra crossings are far apart and motorists frequently ignore them, while in long pedestrian tunnels the person on foot runs the alternative risk of molestation. At a crossroad he must take pot luck. Even when the lights show green for him, most motorists assume they have right of way when turning; if he hesitates too long, the lights change and the cars are off again.

The soft body of a human being has little chance against the hard exterior of a motor vehicle. Some years ago, two American doctors, Hillebore and Larimore, made a detailed study of pedestrians killed in car accidents. After noting the effects in surgical wards and at post mortems, they observed: 'If one were to attempt to produce a pedestrian-injuring mechanism, one of the most theoretically efficient designs which might be developed would closely approach that of the front end of some present day automobiles.'

In Britain, Dr Murray Mackay, of the University of Birmingham Road Accident Research Unit, noted that the high, blunt radiator of a Rolls Royce was more likely to injure a pedestrian than a low one; he would suffer severe chest injuries and be more likely to finish up under the wheels. He proposed that car fronts should be designed with fewer horned features.

Spurred on by belated government legislation, car manufacturers are at last spending money on research and development into making cars safer for occupants. Yet, although nearly a third of road accident casualties are pedestrians, no corresponding weight of effort is happening on their behalf. A cynic might comment that car manufacturers are more concerned with the welfare of the drivers and passengers who constitute their customers than with the unfortunate pedestrians who get in their way.

After his house, his car will be the average man's most

expensive purchase ever; and having bought it, he will pay out another £10 a week to run it. Yet he will have bought an engineering blunder: a machine which is less than five per cent efficient. As a converter of oil into movement, the car's showing is abysmal. John McHale, of the State University of New York, writes in *Futures*: 'Of the energy in crude oil, 13 per cent is lost in refining, 3 per cent in transport to the customer, and 25 per cent is converted to work in the engine; but only 30 per cent of this amount is transmitted to the road (after losses due to friction and auto auxiliaries); and further decreases occur through gears and tyres. The overall efficiency of the automobile is about 5 per cent, though air drag, braking, and idling reduce this in actual operation.'

Basically the modern car is little different from the car of fifty years ago; in the years between, the car manufacturers of the world have put far more effort into marketing than into engineering innovations. Anything which might hasten the car's inevitable journey to the scrap heap, anything that will encourage an owner to trade in for a new one will help achieve the maker's aim of profit and growth. To build a car to cherish, to design a car to last too long would conflict with these aims.

Since a car is a symbol and personality extension, its style is paramount, and must change frequently, even if only in points of detail. Changes in style have been more effective in stimulating sales than significant engineering changes and safety features, and they cost the makers less money. So, for the mass market at least, engineering and safety changes have stayed minimal, and countless drivers, passengers and pedestrians have suffered unnecessarily. Cars have been around for 85 years, yet a million lives have had to be sacrificed before legislation was passed on such an elementary safety measure as the collapsible steering column. To hit another car or an obstacle at 60 mph has the same effect as an unbroken fall face down from a height of 120 feet. Heedless of such comparisons, both industry and public have accepted the obscene concept that in a head-on crash a man's rib cage should collapse in preference to the steering column.

The big three – General Motors, Ford and Chrysler, who make 97 per cent of all cars produced in the US – could have blazed the trail to safer motoring but did not: the customer might baulk at paying more for the benefit, and sales suffer. One study showed that they spent $1.5 billion on restyling in 1969, yet the US Bureau of Labour Statistics estimated that in that year there was no improvement in performance! Styling had become a smokescreen to help protect the '20th century disaster' from being recognized as such; the car manufacturers had shifted from the transport industry to the experience industry – the sizzle had become more important than the steak. William Mitchell, the chief designer of General Motors, said: 'The motor car must be exciting and create a desire, and not become mere transportation, or we will just have a utility and people will spend their money on other things.'

For most driving conditions the shape of the car, derived from styling, is aerodynamically superfluous, while safety is paramount. Yet safety, because it is a poor selling point, has almost invariably yielded to considerations of style. Style sold cars and so style was king. Consumers did not necessarily want change, but the car makers did – desperately – so consumers got it, and paid dearly. The changes, chiefly styling, were a *calculated alternative* to improved safety. Some of the changes actually made cars even less safe – to those outside them as well as those inside.

A classic 'Style versus safety and performance' story is the creation of the best seller Ford Mustang in the US told by Ralph Nader in *Unsafe at Any Speed*. Market research prompted not only the design but the name, for Mustangs are 'wild', and the new, compact car promised status at low cost. The sequence of company events was fascinating: product planners made the basic decisions on the new model and then told the engineers – and for good reason: only the styling features were new; chassis, engine and suspension were merely copies of existing models. Four million

63

people saw the Mustang at dealers when it was launched in 1964 and demand soon outstripped supply. When independent road testers reported on it, however, promises were seen to be no more than promises; performance bore little resemblance to its jumpy name, except that under certain conditions it performed dangerously; the production model lacked at least eight major safety features present in the prototype; style had taken precedence, safety a back seat.

The mass-production car industry in Britain, highly automated and dehumanized, is plagued with labour troubles. Not surprisingly therefore are the findings that, apart from design faults, cars delivered to consumers bristle with construction faults too. In Britain during 1971, the Consumers' Association reported in *Which?* that when they tested 46 cars, none was fault-free, and in all they were delivered to their owners with a total of 588 faults. One car in nine had wrongly adjusted wheel bearings, a defect which could be potentially dangerous. Only a publication such as *Which?* not dependent on car makers' advertising, can be expected to show such objectivity: the rest of the Press mostly run their road tests on shoestring budgets, heavily dependent on co-operation from the car makers, and can be forced to concentrate on performance of the ashtrays. Motoring correspondents feel bitter about this. Said a leader in this field: 'Individual motoring journalists working for newspapers can't criticize like *Which?*, simply because they can't test cars like *Which?* Give us a team of testers, about £1,000 of specialized equipment, and nothing else to do but test drive, and we might.'

No teams of testers or equipment are needed to expose engineering shortcomings, however. For a small extra manufacturing cost, car exhausts could be made to last three times longer and according to Dr T. P. Hoar, corrosion expert at the Department of Trade, if designers cared they could also add two years to the life of bodywork. Cheeseparing such as this saves costs, lures buyers with low prices

64

and boosts turnover by shortening car life. If the motoring Press has been inconspicuous in exposing such practices, the inference may be drawn that it is not in their interest to do so.

Large companies have lost much of the incentive to compete in price, in genuine innovation, in safety, or in quality. The technostructure in their midst, which is at the controls, is committed to diverting consumers' attention from quality, and no single engineer or marketing man of the technostructure any longer has the power within his company to influence it. The technostructure has only a negative incentive to maintain any quality standards: which is based simply on the fact that its company will lose its share of the market if standards fall too low. The key to profits lies in cutting costs, even if to do so shortens the product's life, pollutes the environment and costs human lives.

Champion of safety and arch enemy of exploiters is Ralph Nader, who was given $400,000 and an unqualified apology by General Motors over five years ago for spying into his private life. From a movement specifically to encounter the dangers designed into American cars, the Nader organization has fanned out to embrace many other aspects of consumer protection. He has become a force to be reckoned with, the pioneer of a significant trend. The giant motor companies had to recall over 13 million vehicles to have faults put right – 6.7 million of them in a single recall by General Motors in 1972. He has captured the imagination of the progressives: in the summer of 1970 over 4,000 students volunteered to work for him, though only 200 could be taken on.

In February, 1970, Ralph Nader launched Campaign GM, an unprecedented effort to make General Motors – the world's largest manufacturing corporation – more responsive to social and public need. With its massive size and persuasiveness, General Motors was a leading candidate for the attentions of its consumers, employees, dealers, suppliers, insurance companies and all who suffered its air pollution and other environmental spillages. Through a new organization, Project on Corporate Responsibility, the campaign aimed high, to amend GM's charter so that its business would be limited to purposes not detrimental to public health, safety and welfare. To tell people about GM, the Project circulated a Fact Sheet in 1971 which pointed out that GM alone manufactured almost half the cars on American roads and so was responsible for about 20 per cent of America's air pollution; that of the 55,000 people killed annually on American roads perhaps half were in GM cars, and yet GM opposed adoption of all the government safety standards. In a simulated 5 mph crash a 1971 GM car suffered $367 damage. The campaign continues.

During 1971 Ralph Nader visited Britain and severely criticized the British Government and manufacturers alike for their tardiness over safety. Since Britain had a much higher fatality rate than the US in terms of deaths per vehicle miles travelled – 5.6 deaths per million miles travelled compared with the US figure of 4.9 deaths – Nader declared that British complacency was unjustified. Ralph Nader's chief criticism was simple: British cars sold in the US had certain safety features that were not incorporated in the same cars sold in Britain. 'Are British lives less valuable?' he questioned.

Nader's critics, rising to the defence of British standards, asserted that British manufacturers had concentrated on making cars safer to drive in rather than safer to have an accident in. They pointed out that Britain had pioneered disc brakes and anti-lock devices, developed radial tyres, and concentrated on accurate steering and road holding properties. They forgot to mention, however, the lack of any evidence that performance improvements like the ones selected have in fact reduced accidents. They ignored the well-known 'risk threshold' syndrome in which drivers drive to the limits of their car's handling, tyres and brakes – and then beyond. The British method is characteristic: to be slow to legislate safety standards, so that by enforcement day all major manufacturers will have been using the required designs for years anyway. The introduction of anti-burst door latches is a typical example of this.

Soon after his visit to Britain, Ralph Nader demanded that all Volkswagen Beetles in the US be recalled for extensive safety improvements – his most detailed attack on any one make since his first big success, the halt to General Motors' production of the Corvair. He listed seven charges against the popular Volkswagen, which he called 'the most hazardous car currently in use in significant numbers in the US'. His estimate to make them safe: $182 million. Volkswagen in reply refuted the charges as 'hopelessly out of date'. Yet shortly afterwards the US Government was reported to be considering asking for modifications to Volkswagens as a result.

In mid-1971 the Consumers' Association in Britain departed from normal policy and launched a campaign for safer roads and cars, certain to bring it into open confrontation with both Government and the motor industry. Immediate targets were: compulsory wearing of seat belts, calculated to prevent up to 15,000 deaths and serious accidents a year; mandatory interior padding, plus abolition of all interior rigid projections; braking devices to prevent locking, estimated to save up to 30,000 casualties a year; firm seat anchorages, and stricter overall quality control. Its Chairman, Mrs Jennifer Jenkins, explained the reasons for the campaign: 'The Government has acted too slowly in making compulsory safety features which everyone knows will reduce accidents.'

In the US the Government began a programme of forcing on an unwilling industry safety standards to start taking effect in 1969. By the end of 1971, 36 regulations were on the statute, some already in force, others due to be compulsory on new cars by dates ranging through 1972 and 1973, and one due in 1975. By early 1972, at least 19 of these common sense, life-saving regulations were still not mandatory on British cars made for home use, though they would have to be modified accordingly for export to the US. The 19 missing safety precautions included such elementary protection as: essential controls to be within driver's reach when wearing safety belts; windscreens to have defrosting, defogging systems; emergency dual braking systems; head restraints to save broken necks; firm seat anchorages; fuel tanks designed to cut fire risk; extra roof and side door strength to resist crashes; fire-proof materials for interiors; bumpers to withstand low-speed crashes; retread standards virtually as for new tyres; power-operated windows to be child-proof to avoid self-strangulation in parents' absence; and laceration-free, high penetration-resistant, laminated glass rather than conventional British safety glass.

British cars will have collapsible steering columns and a control to prevent rear displacement of steering columns in a crash – but not until 1972, four years later than in the US!

Manufacturers' excuses for their tardiness are pathetic; they say the safety devices are in manufacturers' standard specifications anyway, and can be bought as optional extras. The British public have a touching faith in their manufacturers and Government to look after their welfare. They are incredulous that profits can be put before lives. As the *New Statesman* said: '. . . we would like to think our capitalists are working for their knighthoods and so would not dare cheat us to make a quick killing.'

Lord Stokes, Chairman of British Leyland, seemed to sum up British car manufacturers' attitudes when he spoke at the 1971 Motor Show. After stating that his company was spending £2 million, a tiny 0.2 per cent of its £1 billion turnover, in dealing with safety and pollution, he explained '. . . it is not possible to accomplish everything we desire overnight. We cannot afford to stop the machine while we do it and we must certainly be very careful not to price the motor car beyond the reach of the average citizen. If we were to do so we would create one of the most galling social injustices one could possibly imagine.'

6 Environmental Rape

THE USA has created an unparalleled colossus: the car industry of Detroit and the highway network on which it runs, made possible by a unique combination of private industry and government.

In 1971 the US had some 85 million cars on the road and about 18 million lorries. In a nation of some 200 million people over 80 per cent of households had at least one car and some 50 per cent had two. There were 85 million cars for 80 million households, and Detroit was planning for a yearly demand ranging from nine to twelve million new cars. Yet in 1971 there was already a vehicle for every 2.1 people, 26 vehicles for every mile of road and a mile of road for each square mile of land. In 1969 direct and indirect expenditure on cars and lorries exceeded $120 billion – twice the expenditure on all forms of education. Each year the figure grows. By 1969 the value of car sales had doubled in just over ten years.

Key to this growth is the US Interstate Highway System, the biggest, most expensive public works project ever undertaken anywhere and the offspring of a most curious and pernicious piece of legislation. Already 33,000 miles long, the US motorways are planned to stretch to 42,500 miles by 1975. By 1970 they had cost $40 billion, and the final bill will be over $76 billion.

The year 1956 was the critical date. Before then a few arterial roads and by-passes – forerunners of the system – existed, but no grand plan. In that year was created both the plan and money to pay for it. The plan was deceptively simple. The Federal Government agreed to pay for

90 per cent of interstate highway costs. The money, which had previously been absorbed into the general revenue from taxes, would come from a specially formed Highway Trust Fund financed by all revenues from Federal taxes on petrol, oil, lorries, buses and caravans, rubber, parts and accessories. This Fund was without precedent and effectively guaranteed the money for all the roads in the plan, which would inevitably be filled, Parkinson-fashion, by Detroit's gargantuan output. It has remained unique in the States. Critics liken its operation to that of diverting all revenue from liquor taxes to improving drinking facilities, or from cigarettes to promoting smoking. With it the Government built the roads – and then promptly washed its hands of them. For although road users may have paid for their *construction*, everybody – road users or not – had to pay, via taxes, for their *maintenance*. The effect of the Fund has been to subsidize Detroit, road hauliers, cement makers, construction companies and all the other industries behind the immensely powerful highway lobby; and also make the nation virtually dependent on one kind of transportation. Predictably, with such financing, railways and buses could not compete, and a rundown of alternative transport methods soon set in.

For a programme as costly and far reaching as the vast, new highway system, some justification had to be found, in case the public should ever query the cost – financial or environmental. After a search the answer was found: 'The system was vital for national defence purposes.' The public swallowed the story and the whole car-highway complex became a beneficiary of the almost unlimited expenditure on defence – in a way not too dissimilar from that of air travel, as we shall see later. Government came forth with the money, industry obliged with the technology: and the American citizen woke up to find he could choose any form of transportation he liked, so long as it was by car. Today 81 per cent of American workers in towns and cities commute by car; only six per cent go by bus and three per cent by train. The rest walk.

The highway system not only sweeps from coast to coast, over ravines, through mountains and across plains; it penetrates the cities themselves. Originally the plan had included by-passes which would be intersected by secondary roads as feeders. The whole stress had been on long distance travel between cities and states, but the lure of Federal Funds to the tune of 90 per cent proved too tempting for local politicians and officials, and before long the tongues of the system were licking hungrily at the gates of cities; in time they entered.

The current disintegration and chaos of US cities is a direct result. Commuters, lorry drivers and interstate travellers converged on to the city centres, roads seized up and the air became polluted. Mesmerized by the fast travel of the early days, city dwellers moved out and created vast, thinly populated new suburbs. Businesses, shops and industries followed them out and city centres began their decline as surrounding country filled up. With no green belt policies, open country receded. Within cities, recreation space was at a premium. Escape from the concrete prison became difficult for those with cars, impossible for those without.

Within cities over 5,000 miles of motorway have already been built and, despite mounting protests from citizens and experts, despite the lessons learned, a further 2,500 are scheduled to open by 1974.

American cities laid waste by urban motorways now have up to a third of their land turned over to the exclusive use of motor vehicles. The motorways devour residential land, parkland, schools, businesses and shops alike. Each huge interchange occupies some forty acres. Side roads are choked with parked and crawling cars. The air is foul and the noise from car engines and horns is incessant. In five years the noise level in American cities has risen 20 per cent. A blueprint for a city designed for machines, but uninhabitable by humans, would closely resemble a large car-dominated US city.

At off-peak times many of the urban motorways can just cope, but in rush hours they seize up. On roads de-

signed for fast traffic the average speed drops to 5 mph.
The wretched commuter, now denied any other form of
travel, must crawl to and from work in a bumper-to-
bumper queue while the subway rider suffers a noisy, filthy
under-capitalized system and the bus traveller joins the
motorists' queue. But the politicians and highway officials
have an answer up their sleeves, and sagaciously act on it:
more roads! So more are built. Road is stacked upon road,
still more land is cleared for fresh roads and extra lanes.
And relentlessly, remorselessly, answering to a seemingly
inviolable law, the traffic increases to fill the extra road
space, so that before long traffic speed falls to its former
crawl. By the 1980s it is expected that weekend congestion
from the leisure boom will be as bad in some places as peak
hour conditions are now on weekdays.

In a nation so committed to free enterprise, planning still
has left-wing connotations and it is not surprising that there
is no national transportation plan. New York has no plan,
and in this it is no exception.

The heart of New York City is Manhattan island where the
surrounding water imposes a singular constraint and the
sky has become the limit on growth. New York's skyline
is a world wonder, breathtaking on first acquaintance even
for the sternest critic, but its beauty is deceptive. Plagued
by the recurrent threats of pollution, power cuts, strikes,
violence, bankruptcy and traffic strangulation, its own
citizens have changed their viewpoint: in one decade awed
admirers of all their city had to offer have become open
critics.

New York has followed the growth pattern of most
large American cities and many others the world over, and
it has done so with classic American hyperbole. In the city
proper, land is chiefly used for business and industry and
for high density housing; what is left over serves for transportation and recreation. Over the years this island centre
has felt the pressures of intense overcrowding: land speculation forced costs up; traffic congestion intensified them;

life became uncomfortable. When the competition for the centre became too intense, commerce, industry and residents started to move out. In time the resultant suburbs acquired the purchasing power to set up satellite centres which competed with the original city, and shops, businesses and industries sprang up all around it.

The original city now undergoes constant change; it becomes increasingly the administrative centre for its expanding hinterland, and only those businesses and shops of hardy economic viability survive. They stand surrounded by areas in various degrees of dereliction.

A city centre, such as New York, can expect to be almost completely rebuilt every 50 years. All this activity, both day-to-day contact and year-to-year regeneration, within a sprawling outer-city, imposes tremendous strains on the original city's radial transportation lines: its traffic problems remain insoluble. In 1906 horsedrawn traffic averaged 11.5 mph in the city centre; by 1966 it was crawling at 8.5 mph, drawn by the world's most powerful mass-produced engines. In 1970, 73,000 New Yorkers walked away from their cars—just left them abandoned in the streets.

A need to go to the same place at the same time is the core of the traffic problem in New York city. Less than eight per cent of the people who work in the city commute by car, but they place an intolerable burden on the city's roads and bridges. Transportation Administration Commissioner, Sidamon Eristoff, would like to improve the standard and availability of public transport to woo these commuters off the roads, but he lacks the cash to do so. 'We are the richest city in the world, but we also have a million on welfare,' he has explained. 'We have vast areas which are totally "bombed out". One and a half million blue and white collar workers have left the city for the suburbs, and their place has been taken by migrants from the South, many of them sharecropper farmers, mostly black, some Puerto Ricans, all ruined by mechanization. Now we are being bled to death by welfare, education and hospitalization payments.'

c*

The commuters are the villains in the piece. The freedom afforded by the car sent them chasing the American
dream of the little house with a little ground – 'it's much
better in the suburbs than those noisy, crumbling city
apartments with the blacks and Puerto Ricans moving in
next door.' Thus most of the city's middle-class working
population now live outside its jurisdiction in New Jersey,
Connecticut and New York State, where they contribute
nothing to the city in rates. Add this to the loss of rates
and taxes from businesses moving out and you have a city
faced with bankruptcy. In 1971 the public transport deficit
was of the order of $150 million. The suburbs are continu-
ing to grow and, despite office building at an unprecedented rate, businesses keep moving out. Population
within the city centre has stayed the same for some 40
years, but its hinterland is expected to grow from 17 to 22
million in ten years. Public transport and plans to humanize
the city compete with other claimants at such a time and
have to take a back seat. Plagued with almost daily crises,
the Administration has made no progress with fully worked
out, integrated transport plans. Along with all its other
problems, New York City's traffic troubles look like getting worse. The city is a grim portent of the dual consequences of unplanned growth and excessive mobility.

If New York is the city without a plan, Los Angeles is the
reverse, and in this respect it is on its own. No other city
resembles it, nor ever will. It is a hymn to the highway,
and the highway is the place where the Angelenos spend
much of their lives. In much of the city up to half the land
is given over to transport use, yet every day brings its
ritual traffic jams. On many days the smog-alert is given,
and children are not allowed to exercise. It has the highest
accident rate in the whole of the US. Less than 70 years ago
it did not exist; there were just huts and desert. Now the
plain that is L.A. is one vast constellation of suburbs sprawling to the mountains, spreading to the surf, joined by
motorways and devoid of public transport, other than air-

buses. Early railways replaced the Spanish military roads that had replaced the Mexican trails. Today's motorways replaced the railways. And that is where Los Angeles is different, for the car is not responsible for this urban caprice. The thin spread of the several centres was ripe for the motorways and the result has been the living sculpture of a flamboyant concrete roller-coaster that is the citizens' alternate curse and joy. Even its neon signs are an essential part of its ambience.

Los Angeles personifies mobility: unashamed in its worship of the god. But the accent is on the means, not the end. In his sprawling city an Angeleno has to go so far to get anywhere that even at 50 mph each journey takes longer than it would in a normal city. And despite the acres of concrete sculpture he suffers the same congestion at peak hours as inhabitants of other large cities. Los Angeles is an example of a city that made up its mind which way to go – and stuck to it. In consequence it is as different from other, older American cities as they are from the cities of Europe. Only America could create Los Angeles; only the car can sustain it; only an Angeleno would wish to live in it. For despite the expense, the world's most fully motorized city barely works.

In 1940, 20 per cent of the American population lived in the suburbs; in 1971 the number had grown to almost 40 per cent – 76 million. Now, with a few exceptions such as New York, where the population is roughly half urban, half suburban, America's suburbs are up to four times more populous than the inner cities they garland.

The suburbs grew up when people moved out to escape from claustrophobic city centres. They worked in the city and slept in the suburb. Groceries might be bought locally, but for special things those living in the suburbs shopped in the city. This has all changed now. Up to 60 per cent of those who sleep in the suburbs also work there and at least half the retail shopping is suburban. Equally significantly, three quarters of the value of new housing construction and two thirds of industrial construction are in the suburbs. These new suburbs are now cities in their own right, for they no longer depend on the inner cities. Typically American, this is the new 'doughnut' development, the outer ring that has emptied the inner city. And in the once-green fields, which suburbia covers, the seeds of the same 'big city' problems are beginning to sprout.

Originally the suburbs clustered round rail routes and radial roads, but when the car freed people from the constraints of trains and buses, the remaining land disappeared and the countryside retreated – taking with it one of the principal reasons for the move. In the 1950s came the first by-passes, or 'beltways' of the massive new highway programme, attracting still more settlement and completing the process of urbanization. The original towns and villages have been submerged in an avalanche of tall hotels, factories, offices, shops and shopping centres and, finally, administrative headquarters. The by-passes have become the accidental main streets of the new cities. They may lack bus station, railway and airport . . . but they have the motorway, the new lifeline.

The car was the catalyst which triggered the Great American Sprawl, but without cheap land and a contempt for planning it could never have happened. With no greenbelts or adequate national parks around cities, upper and middle income families with cars were able to buy extravagantly large plots, and the population spread was thin. If land had been reserved for recreation, forestry and farming, land prices would have been higher, people would have lived closer together and public transport could have worked. There would then have been a viable alternative to the car and more friendly compact living. Douglas E. Kneeland, in the *New York Times*, paints the suburban picture: '. . . all green velvet lawns and swimming pools and two-car garages viewed through picture windows by practising Republicans'.

Not all US suburbs are like this. Acres of little boxes characterize the suburbs of the middle-income bracket and for all their beltway-hugging new centres, the suburbs are still something of a no-man's-land since, being neither city nor country, they lack the cultural inspiration of the city. Despite builders' attempts to mass-produce diversity, there is a dreadful uniformity through every sprawling mile of them and the chase for privacy and greenery becomes increasingly illusory.

Life in the suburbs grows ever more dependent on the car and one per family is not enough. While father uses car number one for commuting, mother uses number two for school trips, week-day shopping and social contact, and junior must have number three for status, for no immobile teenager can hope to hold his own in the suburban sex stakes. Comes Saturday and, on the ritual family social shopping hunt, father encounters the same kind of congestion he may experience all week. Transportation planners, hooked on cars, have overlooked that restless man is also ritual man: everyone wants to do the same thing at the same time, straining all systems, the highways most of all. Without costly land-consuming widening or duplication, they start to seize up. With 'improvement' they quickly attract extra traffic that puts them back to square one.

The shrine of suburbia is the hypermarket shopping centre, now sweeping Europe. Here mobile man comes to worship weekly at the altar of consumerism. The American version is huge – at least 250,000 square feet of shopping space, the main ingredients being department store and supermarket, often in multiples of two, three or four. Shopping centres were planned for one-stop shopping with none of the parking problems of the high street. As they have grown in size and numbers, however, so the problems of parking, traffic congestion and loitering have spread to resemble the chaos of the haphazard high street they set out to replace. Professor Richard Baisden of the University of California is reported to have said of his suburb, Corona del Mar: 'I came here in flight from smog and congestion and I've found relief from both . . . temporarily. I don't know where people will go from here.'

The trouble with the car is that it takes up space. Its noise, its fumes, its murderous potential are all problems capable of a degree of solution, but the space problem is not. A car needs road space merely to stand still, and the faster it moves the more it needs in order to keep a safe distance from the car in front. In Britain there is not land enough for all the space the car demands, nor money enough for the highways – at least not this side of sanity. Nevertheless Britain has already gone a long way towards capitulation to the car. Unmindful of Parkinson's Law and the inevitability that traffic expands to fill the road space available, 'they' are building and planning roads and super roads with a disquieting euphoria.

Between towns the problem is serious; within towns it is critical. To rely on the car as the prime means of transport in towns and cities requires city motorways costing some £12 million a mile and displacing at least 1,000 people for every mile. No fully motorized city functions properly and the further the planners go towards pandering to the car, the worse their problems become.

The planners' attempts to date have been depressing to observe and the prospect ahead for Britain is motorized slums. Compromise has been no solution, for planning has degenerated to the simplified aim of keeping traffic moving and the result has been piecemeal street widening, loss of buildings and amenities, and continuing congestion. So long as cars and lorries have unrestricted access to town and city centres there will be more traffic competing for more space than can be provided. When there were buses and trams on the roads and little else, road space was plentiful and bus travel was fast. But when car ownership grew and people began to travel to work by car because it was faster and more comfortable, road space became scarce, and both cars and buses travelled more slowly. When people began to desert the buses for cars, services became less frequent, so the desertion intensified, and in the end nobody was any better off.

The cost of congestion in Britain has been estimated as something between £500 million and £1 billion a year – borne by the whole community, whether motorist or not. The magnitude of the city congestion problem has been dramatically stated by J. Michael Thomson, Research Fellow in Transport at the London School of Economics. After the Great Fire, the Plague, the Great Depression and the Blitz, London, he writes, 'is now sliding rapidly into what may come to be known as the Great Paralysis'.

Out of the rush hour period London's road system strains like a constipated cow, but a kind of motion *is* achieved. Congestion and a shortage of parking space act as a deterrent and save the system from paralysis. But in peak times the checks are missing on many roads: chaos reigns and traffic crawls. For each day some ten per cent of the commuters in Central London and 20 per cent in outer London block with their cars the passage of all those who go by bus.

The private motorist shares the blame for congestion, noise, vibration and exhaust pollution with his fellow road-user, the freight haulier. During the last century, railways took over from canals the task of moving the bulk of the nation's freight: in this century it is the turn of the roads to replace rail, and the past decade has been characterized by a steady transfer from rail wagon to lorry. Between 1960 and 1969, the percentage of total ton-miles carried by road rose from 48 to 59 per cent, while rail fell from 30 to 20 per cent. Britain is the only country in Europe where the volume of rail freight has fallen; everywhere else it has risen.

Some environmental damage must result from any large scale movement of goods, but the damage incurred by using railways is unmistakably lower than that caused by using roads. One train of only 14 wagons can move the same amount of oil as 30 huge 44-ton vehicles. Lorries invade pedestrian-filled high streets and thunder within feet of hospitals and private homes, but railways, though far

79

from perfect, run further from homes and the noise per ton moved is far less. Road freight creates more air pollution than rail and requires five times more energy per ton mile. Yet Britain's roads, towns and cities, so demonstrably unsuited to monstrous lorries, each year become more crowded with them. In 1960 there were 10,000 vehicles over eight tons unladen weight; by 1968 there were 40,000. And in same period payloads progressively increased to the 1972 permitted maximum of 32 tons. Payloads are likely to increase again. At the 1971 Conservative Party Conference, the Minister of Transport Industries admitted that the weight limit, which puts British hauliers at a disadvantage with their European rivals, would have to be reviewed before very much longer. If it is, taxpayers will have to part with £200 million for strengthening roads and bridges. So long as road freight escapes from paying its true cost to the economy by ignoring noise, ground vibration, air pollution and other damaging effects and so long as the public remains apathetic, the growth trend will continue.

In 1971 the Greater London Development Plan was unwrapped and exposed to a public enquiry. Its most controversial point was the proposal to solve the congestion problem by building £1.8 billion of motorways with an inner ringway skirting the city proper and running through densely populated suburbs. Thousands of sound houses would simply disappear. The hostility to these proposals was widespread and typical of criticism wherever motorways threaten to displace people from their homes and divide close-knit communities, and opposition was concentrated in the quickly formed Hampstead Motorway Action Group. This paved the way for a full-scale professional campaign by the London Motorway Action Group, which stressed the effects that the inner ringway would have on London's already acute housing shortage.

It is estimated that between 60,000 and 100,000 people would lose their homes through the proposals – this total could even rise to 120,000. Yet there were already about

570,000 Londoners needing adequate homes, and the whole-sale destruction of homes proposed would only prolong the waiting time for them. It was completely misleading to suggest that, because people displaced by a motorway would be rehoused, housing conditions generally would get no worse. The main limiting factor, as the GLG itself had pointed out, was already a lack of land. Yet land lost to motorway construction would be land lost for housing. The people displaced would have to occupy land which could otherwise have rehoused those already in need. The inner ringways would require no less than 6,200 acres or 9.7 square miles. But this only accounted for people directly displaced. Situated just beyond them were many more whose quality of life would suffer through noise, vibration and pollution, and these people would get no compensation at all. Nowhere did the GLC Plan aim to house all its citizens; capital expenditure on housing would remain constant while expenditure on roads escalated.

When all costs were taken into account the proposed £1.8 billion would in fact exceed £2.4 billion excluding compensation. This was the most costly peacetime public investment project ever proposed in Britain – as large as, if not larger than, the British share of the Concorde, Channel Tunnel and Third Airport put together; yet still a regional project not a national one. The London Motorway Action Group declared that the project would involve an excessive investment in roads over houses and would prolong for many years ahead the acute distress that the lack and bad quality of housing caused.

Westway carves its way into West London, and ends at a set of traffic lights. It is a motorway designed as if to clog – and clog it does, repeatedly, though without warning, with traffic queues up to a mile long. Of all examples of callous indifference to human needs this project was the worst: at some points it ran only 11 feet away from bed-room windows. Not until residents organized themselves and planned a campaign of disruption to traffic on the motorway did the GLC reluctantly reverse its policy of indifference and provide new homes at once for the 117 families most severely affected.

In Covent Garden, where 96 acres of central London have been earmarked for development with the end of the vegetable market, people who have lived all their lives as members of a tightly knit community will be forced out by high rents. The plans provide for a system of wide carriageways, including an enlarged Charing Cross Road and a new sunken road. Always the pious hope that more roads equal less congestion . . .

Loss of homes and amenities is not confined to London. Throughout Britain, cities and towns are grappling with the problem of worsening congestion and too often the answer is outright capitulation to the car. Despite the grim evidence of America, city fathers still fail to recognize that roads *attract* traffic: new roads and wider roads provide no more than temporary alleviation before congestion returns to its former level. Oxford is one such city. A scheme which would introduce eight miles of major road was considered in 1971, involving the destruction of strongly built Edwardian terrace houses and the community spirit in districts through which the roads would cut a swathe. The scheme has been seen as the ruination of the ancient city just so that cars can enter and pass through. Yet about half of Oxford's households have no car! In Cambridge a proposed bypass scheme has also been attacked. According to critics it would pass too close to Girton College and the village of Girton would be cut in half. In Bristol a plan to take the Parkway through the poor, multi-racial district of St Pauls has also been severely criticized. Houses have already been razed, not to make way for desperately needed new housing but for roads. Good houses have been destroyed, businesses closed and large sections of the remaining community made impotent while the threat of disintegration hangs over them.

This is the growing curse of 'planning blight' – the fate of areas where demolition schemes are expected, but not yet finally agreed. Since no one wants to buy property in

ENVIRONMENTAL RAPE

a threatened area its value slumps. Then, when compensation is finally agreed, it probably reflects not the original value but its worth after years of uncertainty. In 1971 the Law Society recognized the injustice of the situation and recommended that people affected should be able to get compensation from the planning authority or oblige it to buy their property.

Cardiff has planned a Los Angeles-style highway to its centre, the 2½-mile Cardiff Hook Road, estimated to cost some £30 million and passing through closely settled suburbs. 1973 will be the earliest possible starting date, *if* the plan survives an enquiry and gets government consent. For two years at least 1,500 houses will have suffered 'planning blight' yet may never be pulled down. Meanwhile desperate residents have sold out at knock-down prices or offered their homes for sale to prove to the Council they are unsaleable.

The 1971 Census showed that between 1961 and 1971 Britain's population increased five per cent, to 55 million; in the same period the number of cars increased 100 per cent to 12 million. During the decade, although the total population went up, London lost 600,000 people. Liverpool and Manchester lost proportionately more and in Birmingham, Glasgow, Nottingham, Leeds and Sheffield the same trend was evident. Commenting on this, *The Times* wrote: 'Growth of the car population and dispersal of human population feed each other. Car ownership pushes people out of expensive, densely populated city centres into outer areas where there is more room and more scope for cars.'

Some people find encouragement in the decay of the heart of a great city. In picturing a city they see congested streets and lack of parks; office buildings and factories cheek by jowl with rows of mean houses: a place of incessant noise and foul smell. And the car becomes to them the Great Liberator. But there is another side of the coin. As *The Times* stated: '. . . congestion of the right amount at the right times is of the essence of a city. City centres are

83

by definition scenes of coming together of people. Yet some are not. Some, like the City of London, are emptied by night of commuters who fill the offices by day.' A city heart, which consists principally of offices, factories, places of culture, entertainment and exhibition, does not beat healthily. It needs people who live there, who do so, not from desperation but from choice; for as people with money to run a car move out, their place is taken by immigrants. Houses designed for one family become 'multi-occupancy' houses with inadequate facilities, and new arrivals have a tough time finding work and becoming integrated.

Many people working in the social services fear that these under-privileged families will be the inhabitants of a new generation of ghettoes. They are destined to become poorer, while the suburbanites and 'new town' dwellers, whose place they filled, grow richer. This trend to poverty is seen as a very real possibility, despite Government and local authority programmes of extra expenditure on social services, which do not go far enough.

The Census in fact failed to reveal the full extent of the exodus from the cities: since immigrants gravitate to them, the numbers of original citizens who have left is greater than the total figures suggest. Money which might be spent in re-creating city hearts is spent instead on feeding the nation's insatiable appetite for mobility and the policy seems to be 'Roads before Homes'. In consequence, the cities, which might have been forums for intellectual and cultural ideas, degenerate into commercialism; and the countryside which might have kept its agriculture, its beauty and tranquillity, melts away under a thinly spread population of motorized suburbanites and the massive network of roads built to serve them. Isolated as bus services run down, ever more dependent on the car, the people who live there are discovering the Loneliness of the Long Distance Suburb.

Each year 100,000 acres of Britain's countryside are lost to new houses, industrial sites and roads. Mass mobility poses a triple threat to this dwindling natural resource: city-to-city motorways, suburban sprawl and mass intrusion of people from towns. The first is dramatic – inescapable in its visual insults, whereas the second spreads slyly – destructively creeping out from the centre like molten lava.

With the coming of the motorway, quiet villages within reach of an intersection have become the centres of a new 'creeping sprawl'. Estate agents bristle, land prices rise, pubs are tarted up, new estates develop, swallowing developing farmlands. Rownhams in Hampshire, population 600, was one village to suffer. The official route of the M27 was planned to run through it, demolishing several houses, cutting land off others, and isolating part of the village from the rest. The excuse was that it would be too expensive to route the motorway half a mile to the north of the village. As if this were not enough, villagers were told of plans to site a service area with restaurant astride the motorway barely 100 yards from the village. Along with the local councils they objected, but the Minister chose not to hold a public enquiry.

The Lake District has been threatened by 23 miles of major 'improvements' to the A66: a historic area near Winchester in Hampshire has faced rape in an extension of the M3; the National Trust masterpiece, Petworth Park in Sussex, has been confronted with ruinous dismembering from a by-pass . . . the list of recent threats is long, but in comparison with the list to come if the next 2,000 miles of main roads gets going, it will one day seem short. The ensuing loss of land might conceivably be justified if the new roads conferred true social benefit. But the same syndrome operates in the country as in towns and cities: more roads simply attract more traffic. The case of the Doncaster By-pass Motorway illustrates the point; after it was opened, traffic on both the motorway and the old road which it replaced increased 30 per cent! Previously the old road had carried 29,000 vehicles a day; the motorway now carried 14,000 and the old road was still carrying nearly 24,000.

85

Because of Britain's green belts and planning procedures the country may be spared the worst effects of the 'doughnut development' of the US but nevertheless 'sprawlurbia' is already a fact and is fast spreading. Instead of the old, compact form of towns and cities, large areas of 'no-man's-land' take shape, neither town nor country. Scarce farm and recreation land is lost, not only as building plots, but as the stretched network of roads needed to serve it. And into this new life style comes the extra intrusion of the hypermarket, the American importation and property developer's dream which has already swept France and West Germany. A few have already appeared in Britain, but the flood was being held back during 1972 while the Minister of State for the Environment made up his mind on a policy. At first sight the developers' arguments seem convincing: instead of a slow drive to the congested high street with parking problems and long walks between shops and car, the family has a fast, easy ride, usually on a motorway, to free parking at a one-stop centre where a vast selection of goods is sold at a discount. But there is another aspect: hypermarkets are strictly for car owners, still a minority, and as they spread so amenities for non-car families deteriorate. As small, high street shops lose business, town centre decay is aggravated, and the spontaneous human contact that characterizes 'old fashioned' shopping is lost, to be replaced by sterile uniformity. Hypermarkets encourage the need for still more roads, and as other developments follow them out into the dwindling countryside, more and more precious land is lost to recreation and farming.

In the 'scattered districts' which now engulf the countryside, public transport cannot function properly, and to reach shops, clubs and entertainment, residents must depend entirely on the car – for activities to which they would once have walked. Today they are no more mobile; they have merely put themselves in a situation where they have to travel further for the same effect.

Over the years suburban sprawl has been steadily growing in one other singularly unobtrusive way: the second home for weekends and holidays. In a report published early in 1972 the National Trust expressed anxiety about 'the relentless pressure for second homes which is ousting the natives'. Under the pressures of life in an industrial society, and motivated by the deterioration of city living which the car has brought about, more and more people are buying 'a place to get away to'. The result is an increase in traffic and still more erosion of countryside and its character.

The third threat to the countryside – mass intrusion – is no less grave. The town dweller seeks to escape to the country and seashore for quiet and beauty but when he gets there he finds himself surrounded by fellow urbanites, noise and visual squalor. In particular, Britain's national parks are now feeling the pinch. The way things are going they will soon become National Car Parks! In the New Forest alone there are 3½ million day visitors a year; people drive their vehicles onto the heath and sward, to picnic and to camp, killing the grass and causing soil erosion. As a result the birds are leaving and wild flowers are rarer. The picture is similar wherever areas of natural beauty lie close to towns or motorways.

The Ramblers' Association deplores the widening of rural roads to ease the problem: widening takes away the very beauty the traveller has set out to see. As far back as 1934, 11,000 visitors signed a petition against widening roads in the Lake District, but in vain. Many people would like to see cars banned altogether from national parks, but when plans were drawn up to keep cars out of parts of the Lake District, the scheme was abandoned because of protests.

However, many motorists are at last starting to see sense. A 1969 survey on the Yorkshire Dales found that two-thirds of motorists visiting beauty spots thought them over-crowded. In Derbyshire Peak District an experiment to reduce weekend congestion in 1970 has succeeded: motorists to the Goyt Valley, where cars were excluded, took happily to free mini-buses, and over 90 per cent of those surveyed approved the scheme.

Often the trouble spot is not a park but a single place of beauty or interest. Stonehenge cannot keep its magic in competition with near-by ice-cream vans, complete with chimes, and even if such free enterprise were banned the official car park underpass and cafeteria still threaten its mystique. One solution proposed is to move the car park, or put it underground, and limit the number of visitors somehow.

With mass-intrusion comes litter pollution, a problem that has taken on a new, ugly turn since food and soft drink manufacturers began using plastic containers and non-returnable bottles. Two new menaces have arrived: a sharp rise in injuries from broken glass and the prospect of permanent litter pollution. By the end of 1972 throwaway soft drink bottles will be produced at the rate of 450 million a year, and new plastics, unlike former materials, are virtually indestructible. A spokesman for Canada Dry has put the industry viewpoint: clearly 'Manufacturers are not going to get involved in paying social costs unless they have to.' Which is vaguely reminiscent of the attitude of the car industry . . .

7 Whatever Happened to Buses and Trains?

America

As car numbers have grown, public transport* has shrunk. In most industrial states companies that ran public transport have run into the red and either been nationalized or liquidated. A study of events in the US and Britain throws light on the causes of this. First let us take a look at the contestants in the transport war: The plane competes with the train within a critical band determined by time and distance; up to a few hundred miles trains are faster and cheaper, but for the next few hundred the two modes compete; after that planes win on speed, leaving rail to those for whom cost – and perhaps scenery – are important considerations.

The real war is the car versus bus and train, for each offers the traveller advantages of speed, comfort, safety, flexibility and cost in varying degrees. And each imposes strains on society and the environment in varying degrees. In America the car has won the first battle, but mighty resources are rapidly being marshalled behind its adversaries. Once again, the US offers lessons for the rest of the world, now learning the costs and hardships of this particular war.

Until 1971 the mammoth national task of moving 200 million Americans in and between towns was attempted

* Although air travel and taxis are also 'public transport', for simplicity the term throughout refers to buses and trains, excluding air travel and not necessarily including taxis.

without a plan. Then, at last the Department of Transportation produced one—the Balanced Transportation Plan— balanced in the sense that highway construction and car production continued unabated, the self-financing Highway Trust Fund remained sacred, and railways and buses received belated Government handouts.

According to many critics, the attempt to formulate some kind of plan has happened too late and so has little chance of success. One of the sternest critics is Willie L. Brown, Jnr., Chairman of the Ways and Means Committee of the California State Assembly, who maintains that the design of equipment for moving people has been determined, not by the people who must use it, but by the needs of the makers —in other words the technostructure. The makers decided the kind of highways. 'The location of highways has never been designed around people,' he insists. 'This is because the makers of vehicles contribute heavily in terms of visible support, financial and otherwise, to the election of those who pass the legislation which effects such things. The oil companies are part of a vast power-block which makes people believe that the economy cannot exist without transportation being dictated by makers rather than users. The decisions are made, then sold to the users as a packaged deal.' He sees the Highway Lobby as the culprit. Minorities – the handicapped, the poor, the aged – should get together and expose the power of the Lobby, he urges. Wherever this has been done, the Lobby has lost. 'The change in attitude, which is required to ensure that minorities are represented in the nation's transportation plans, represents a change of attitude of the same order as the change over Vietnam,' he insists. 'It is a political matter, not just an educational one – a very hot political potato.'

The US Secretary of Transportation, John A. Volpe himself, has admitted that the nation has not been successful in planning for people. 'By building a wonderful highway system', he said in 1971, 'we have done much to accommodate the motor car, but often to the detriment of the Nation's public transit systems. Our civil aviation developments made air transportation popular and proficient, but at the cost of reduced rail patronage and the near-demise of passenger train services.'

Ralph Nader has no time for 'doubletalk': he attributes the failure of the US transportation system fairly and squarely to the existence of the alternative, more profitable, highway system.

The highway programme, financed from the Highway Trust Fund, laid down the tracks for the cheap mass-produced products of Detroit to run on, while the railway companies watched their privately financed tracks go to rust, and the bus companies saw their vehicles snarled up in the jams created by their competitors.

Nevertheless, observers who insist that there is no future for public transport in the US have overlooked some important statistics. Despite the country's great distances and the spread of its suburban sprawl, the average car trip is only nine miles long, and most trips occur within a 25-mile radius of metropolitan areas. The significance of these figures is clear: in many areas, population densities are high enough to support public transport systems, if only they were available, and if only people would fall out of love with their cars. Ironically, the largest makers of buses in the world are also the world's greatest car makers – General Motors. With cars their major profit earner and buses a threat to cars, the initiative is unlikely to come from that quarter.

Eighty per cent of Americans live in towns comprising a mere two per cent of the land area, and ninety-four per cent of all travel in urban areas is by car. It used to be different. Public transport patronage is only a quarter what it was after World War Two and it is still falling.

In 1970 there occurred the worst collapse in the history of modern US business – the 6 billion dollar Penn-Central railway bankruptcy. The affair had all the drama of a major accident and the world's headlines responded faithfully. Almost unreported however was the stream of closures that preceded it. In 1929 the US had 20,000 inter-city passenger trains; in April 1971 the number was down to 366 with plans for a further reduction to 165. Rail freight, however, boomed and proved profitable, but this only contributed to the passenger decline. Railway companies transferred their efforts to this one profitable sector and so hastened the demise of the other one. Finally they made a deal with the Government which left them with the still profitable freight business while the Government assumed responsibility for passengers with a service called Amtrak.

The erosion of public transport services has hit the whole community. Every non-motorist is made daily aware of his consequent immobility. The young, the old, the handicapped and the poor are the ones to suffer most. In 1966, the source of serious riots in Los Angeles was traced to anger over lack of transport. An investigating commission found that people experienced difficulty in seeking and holding jobs, attending schools, shopping, and fulfilling other needs. 'It has had a major influence in creating a sense of isolation, with its resultant frustration,' the Commission reported.

The great American freeway is anything but free. In a wealthy country whose eccentric economy deprives its people of their just share in its wealth, many families cannot afford a car. With 20 million Americans in the poverty bracket, it is not surprising that 20 per cent of the families do not own a car, and in some places such as Washington the capital, the percentage rises to 50. Proponents of the car forget that 65 million Americans are under 16 years of age and 20 million are over 65. In all it has been estimated that up to 30 per cent of the population depend on trains and buses; they are too poor to own a car, too old or too young to drive, or have a physical handicap which prevents them from driving.

At a Transportation Conference in Washington, D.C. in 1971, citizens' groups representing minorities testified passionately for an alternative system to the car. The mockery of Medicare was cited: sick people could not afford the cab fare to get to hospital for free treatment. Desperate people were prevented from working: commuter fares could total $2 a day – prohibitive on a salary of 3,000 to 5,000 dollars. Half the nation's one million handicapped, homebound persons were kept unemployed for lack of transport. Finally, in July 1971 the aged and handicapped received recognition: $693,000 dollars from the Department of Transportation for projects to improve their lot – yet expenditure on the 1971 space programme totalled three billion dollars.

In the US demands from citizens for a pluralistic transport system, designed for people rather than machines, are mounting. The US Government, finally recognizing in its midst a fully fledged market failure, has addressed itself to the need to revitalize the dying alternatives to the car, and give consumers 'freedom of choice' in travel. Hence the plan for 'balanced transportation', officially described as one in which all modes complement one another, rather than duplicate or compete. The plan hopes to offer flexibility of travel from an urban area to any other place at any time of day – not merely in rush hours – for non-commuters and for reverse commuters (those who live in town and work in suburbs). It would also embrace freight.

In 1970, the Government passed the Urban Mass Transportation Act which promised $10 billion over 12 years to make public transport efficient, comfortable, fast and safe. Significant amounts of local funds, however, are still necessary to generate public transport improvements; its success largely depends on wooing drivers away from the cars they love. Although the Highway Trust Fund will operate until 1977 to maintain this beautiful relationship, John Volpe displayed a marked change of viewpoint when, in March 1972, he finally heeded citizens' demands and proposed that $1 billion be released from the Fund in 1974 and used for urban public transport or highways.

Champions of public transport have plenty going for them: congestion both on the roads and in the air is getting worse; rail tracks already exist – they are relatively cheap to upgrade for fast travel, and no more land need be eaten up. (New York's two mainline termini handle 105 million passengers a year on 124 acres; its three airports handle a third as many on 60 times more land); rail is the safest of all transport modes; it operates in all weathers and penetrates to the heart of towns and cities. On so many counts public transport wins hands down. Take safety: trains are one-and-a-half times safer than buses, two-and-a-half times safer than planes, and 23 times safer than cars. Or fuel economy: trains are 12 times more efficient per passenger-mile than cars, and buses five times more efficient. Or congestion: one traffic corridor 12 feet wide, equal to one highway lane, can carry the following number of passengers an hour: 3,600 by car, 42,000 by train or 60,000 by bus (assuming realistic carrying capacities per vehicle, realistic speeds, realistic distances between them).

Trains and buses now have a chance. More to the point, the American public has a chance too – even those outside, or on the fringe of the economic system, the poor, handicapped, young and old. But it will remain an *outside* chance as long as politicians and planners continue to hold out against mounting pressure from concerned citizens and avoid the red hot issue of curbing the car. Until then, however much money is pumped into public transport from the public purse, 'balanced transportation' will amount to little more than a political tranquillizer and the expensive lessons of the US will continue to be available free to the rest of the world.

Britain

The picture in Britain closely resembles the USA. Public transport, except for Inter-city rail services, is a depressed, unglamorous industry, dependent on handouts for survival. In ten years, buses have lost a quarter of their passengers, and on present trends fleets will be halved in the next ten years. On the railways, 4,500 miles of passenger routes have been axed and more closures are likely.

The private car is again the culprit: in the absence of

any national plan to move Britain's 55 million people, the car has become the rogue elephant in a transport jungle. In towns and cities, car travel has slowed to a crawl, bringing buses, taxis and lorries down to the same level; in the country, car ownership by a minority has forced bus companies to cut services for the majority. Four million country people are threatened; scores of villages are already isolated.

The story begins with the railways. In 1962 when the Conservative government appointed Lord Beeching, then Dr R. Beeching, a businessman, as chairman of British Railways, his brief was to make British Rail pay – to wipe out the loss then running at £134 million a year. The railways were examined in total isolation from the transport needs of the country as a whole, and without consideration for the needs of those for whom there was no alternative form of satisfactory transport. The action for which Dr Beeching has qualified for a place in the history books, is his railway closures. By the end of 1965, when he returned to industry, he had closed down 176 services, 1,145 stations and 2,289 passenger route miles.

After the Beeching Era, rail closures still continued. From the beginning of 1966 to the end of 1970, 112 services and 1,789 passenger route miles were withdrawn, and 738 stations were closed. In 1968, British Rail was divided by Act of Parliament into two parts: a self-supporting commercial railway, comprising chiefly the profitable Intercity network; and a grant-aided social service railway comprising the London and provincial commuter services, cross-country city-to-city services and the 'green fields' lines – those surviving the Beeching-and-after axing. Closures still take place because the grants of around £60 million a year have been insufficient to meet rising costs. Future grants will almost certainly be pegged – and their value further eroded by uncontrollable cost increases; but British Rail say that if a mere two per cent a year in real terms were added to a total grant which kept pace with inflation, *there would never need to be another closure!*

The health of British Rail is linked with a satisfactory solution to the freight problem – a factor it shares with the environment. Although, as we have seen, Britain's roads are unsuited to carrying the nation's freight, rail has steadily lost out to them. Unfortunately the dice are loaded against the railway, for not only does road transport enjoy vast, hidden subsidies, it also has, at present, a cost advantage over short distances. In Britain the average length of freight haul is only 70 miles, but rail scores best on longer distances: a study in 1966 showed that 67 per cent of all freight tonnage went under 25 miles and only nine per cent went over 100 miles. Moreover, the railway system now runs on less than 12,000 miles, in contrast to 200,000 miles of road network. From 1960 to 1969 the freight system decreased by 6,300 miles, and the more it shrinks the less well it can compete.

Britain's inadequate road system now carries three-quarters of all inland goods. The demand for all transport – passenger and freight – is expected to rise by two thirds in the next 15 years and the system will be grossly over-strained as the railway system is under-used. As British Rail has pointed out: 'This level of demand is bound to overtake the expedients so far used to cope, more or less successfully, with the situation – road improvements and larger vehicles.' In the context of such massive growth in passenger and freight traffic, the concept of closing down developed rail routes, while spending taxpayers' money on new roads, has a naïve ring of logic. If the one-time rail passenger, now a motorist running his own individual transport system, ever has to pay the true cost of such excessive mobility, he will clamour to lay down again the tracks which were torn up so hurriedly in the interests of commercial tidiness.

British Rail sees lack of investment finance as the main obstacle to pleasing customers and improving its bad public image. The scale of Exchequer handouts goes nowhere near to solving this problem. It resents the £1,000 million lavished on Concorde and the annual £550 million on main roads, while it can embark on investment programmes of only

£100 million a year. As Richard Marsh, chairman of British Rail, has said: '. . . in comparison with road expenditure, railways do not receive a fair share of the cake. As a proportion of total public expenditure, rail investment in 1970 was 0.4 per cent while the road figure was 2.6 per cent. In 1974 the figures will be 0.5 per cent and 3.1 per cent!'

British Rail has stressed its advantage over road and air travel in environmental terms. Railways, it says, make little visual intrusion, cause virtually no pollution, use land more economically and make less noise. 'By using rail for inter-city journeys, people not only add to their own comfort and avoid personal strain, they also avoid harming the environment for hundreds of thousands of others whom they would have polluted and congested on the way, if they had used their own personal transport.'

Britain's 59 million acres support a population of over 56 million. By the year, 2,000 it may rise to 66 million. This means finding space for nine more cities the size of Birmingham, using six million acres of countryside in the process. In this context British Rail emphasizes its land economies. A mile of motorway can absorb up to 40 acres, but the railways are already there. If people are to travel *individually*, acres of good land must be sterilized for ever. 'The individual solution – every adult person, and every sizeable unit of goods, to have its own engine and wheels – cannot go on working much longer.'

The Beeching railway closures had isolated rural communities all over the country. To help them the Government set up extra bus services, British Rail subsidizing them as necessary. Yet as the sixties rolled on, buses too began to run into serious trouble. Rural services had not paid their way, but their losses had traditionally been made good by profits from city services and these profits were dwindling. During the sixties the nation had been radically changing its life style: car ownership doubled from 5.5 million to over 11 million; television licence numbers jumped 50 per cent, and 48 million viewers stayed at home; while the five-day week became general. All this added up to less bus travel.

In 1967 the Labour Government published a White Paper aimed at arresting the decline in public transport. One of its plans was to set up a National Bus Company, backed by Government grants, with the brief to improve bus services and make them pay. Mrs Barbara Castle, then Minister of Transport, declared that there were two ways of tackling the problem: one was to provide a standby service with a minimum of facilities for those without cars. She said: 'I call this the cattle truck philosophy and I reject it. I have opted for what I call the Pullman philosophy, enabling it to provide a service which demonstrably competes with the private car in efficiency, comfort, reliability and general attractiveness.' The National Bus Company set up shop on January 1st 1969, but soon found itself saddled with an impossible brief; a year later it ordered its subsidiaries to withdraw all the rural services making heavy losses, unless Councils would make good the losses out of rates. Councils, despite a 50 per cent contribution from the Exchequer, showed little interest, and bus services began to disappear all over the country – even where the Beeching axe had fallen earlier. The Government stepped in with a loan of up to £6 million to tide over the National Bus Company which then revealed an operating loss for 1970 of £5.1 million – over £3 million below budget.

By this time the ruthless Beeching formula was being practised by the National Bus management. The car and rising costs had made the company's original brief impossible. The design of buses had been virtually unchanged for thirty years, but lack of investment capital dashed any hopes of changing rural buses to meet the demands of the seventies and compete. The buck had to stop somewhere: where else but on the doorstep of the country dweller, whose services were axed?

The amount of money required to keep rural bus services solvent would have been small in comparison with other public expenditure on transport, but by mid-1971 the

Government's abdication became total. It sent a letter to country and rural district councils saying in effect that from then on rural buses would only play a limited role. Those without cars would have to beg lifts from their more fortunate neighbours, and 'Parish Councils or local voluntary groups could help by acting as clearing houses'. There were enough cars to go round, the Government maintained: what was needed was a 'measure of good neighbourliness'. To circumvent existing regulations, the Government made new proposals exempting cars and mini-buses from road service licensing, so that owners would be able to give lifts for payment. Announcing this, Mr Peyton, Minister of Transport Industries, said that the changes were the result of 'a crisis in public transport caused by the tremendous and engulfing wave of private cars'. The penny had taken a long time to drop, for across the Atlantic the lesson was there for the learning. Britain had steered the same course, yet when she suffered the same fate, the Minister was taken by surprise. The scheme pinned its hopes on minibuses, ignoring the fact that they had been discounted in two of the Government's own studies and rejected by bus companies for their high operating cost per passenger.

With a dying public transport service, the general drift to over-crowded towns and cities intensified, for a new under-privileged rural class had been created: people without access to a car. Nearly 42 per cent of the ten million people who lived in places served by country buses now had no personal transport except perhaps a bicycle. In just four years, four million people saw Barbara Castle's 'Pullman passenger' dream replaced by a hitch-hiker reality.

In towns and cities, the bus picture of the sixties was not much rosier. Between 1960 and 1969, the number of passenger journeys made by London's central buses fell by over 30 per cent. In 1970, London Transport's buses lost £3.5 million, and in the following year the Board raised fares 8 per cent. The GLC reported: 'With the steady increase in car ownership in Greater London, this trend is bound to continue.' Now a question mark hangs over the future of London's buses. One of the first pronouncements of the newly formed London Transport Executive was that 'Unless means are quickly found of reducing drastically the operating costs of buses, it will not be a question of reducing frequencies and reshaping services, but of closing down completely large numbers of services.'

The great majority of Londoners do not enjoy exclusive use of a car. In 1966 over five-sixths of Greater London's population were in this unenviable category, and even by 1981 the proportion is likely to be reduced to three-fifths, while in Inner London the proportion is even higher. For all these people the decline of the bus is no mere inconvenience, it is nothing less than a deprivation of their capacity to get to work, to make essential calls and to enjoy life.

In provincial cities and towns the story is the same. In 1971, the largest independent operator, Midland Red, which serves Birmingham, the Black Country and beyond, and is part of the National Bus Company, fired 650 of its 7,500 workers after reporting losses the previous year of nearly £700,000. Yet in that year it had run a recruitment campaign featuring long-term job prospects!

Late in 1971, rather than attack the basic cause of the problem and plan nationally, the Government indulged in more cosmetic surgery and allocated two grants: £18 million to improve train and bus services in towns, and £35 million to hold down fare increases and keep rail and bus services out of the red during 1972. Almost at once the GLC approved yet another fare increase on buses and tubes – this time up to 100 per cent and the forerunner to further swingeing increases in less than a year.

The rampant inefficiencies of the bus's and train's competitor, private road transport, are masked by direct and hidden subsidies. Inefficiency, however, is catching and spreads: private road transport siphons passengers from rail and bus services, forcing them to raise fares, cut services and become even less competitive. And every cut generates more candidates for the private car which destroys the city scene. In the decade ending passenger journeys by bus fell by a third, while car use soared by a third.

To win back the lost passengers buses must be reliable and fast, but they cannot be so while cars reduce progress to horse and buggy speed. At peak times, when buses could be most use, car thrombosis is at its worst: a traffic lane of private cars can carry only about 1,000 passengers; a bus lane ten times as many. When private cars jam public roads buses become slow, irregular and unpopular – and governments watch helplessly. In time, however, they find themselves forced to act, and do so by unimaginatively doling out financial aid. The taxpayer by then is committed to a double handout: one to private road transport and another to public transport – neither of which runs efficiently.

8 Planning for People

The car has caused the run-down of buses and trains, and as services deteriorate, so it becomes more of a necessity. This run-down is precisely what the car manufacturers need as an extra boost to turnover – and they know it. In Britain, the Government knows it too, and, in consequence, it vacillates in a state of neurotic indecision on transport policy. Into this void the planners rush headlong, obsessed with predicting traffic volumes due to growing car ownership, and concentrating on the needs of car owners so that the necessary roads can be built to serve them. Because the car has a way of dazzling people, because it is part of the technological exponential and because whole industries directly and indirectly depend on it, the planners know that private road transport can attract the funds they demand and that people will accept the idea that the car is the answer to the problem of moving people around.

Transport planners seem to assume that everyone has or will soon have a car. But only 20 per cent of the population now has *exclusive* use of one, and even by the year 2000 the proportion will be still only 40 per cent. The rest of the population must get about as best they can: where there is a car in the household all those who cannot drive must forgo their independence and, with luck, be chauffeured by some other, often unwilling member of the family. But nearly half the households in Britain have no car, so every one of their members must rely on a dwindling, increasingly expensive public transport system, or else travel on foot in an environment which the car makes less and less conducive to walking: polluted with fumes, ugly and

cluttered with parked cars and street furniture, and demonstrably dangerous. Moreover, since the car encourages
sprawl, *everyone* must travel further to satisfy essential
needs of work, shopping and social contact.

The hardships inflicted by planning myopia were described to a special parliamentary committee in 1972 by Dr
Mayer Hillman, a planner specializing in the problems
of personal mobility. Car ownership was concentrated in
the upper, middle and younger social strata, he stressed.
Nine tenths of elderly people's households had no
car, nor did nearly three quarters of the lowest third
income group. 'This is simply because the optional use of
a car is dependent on three prerequisites – adequate age,
income, ability to hold a licence and run a car.' And on
present trends, in thirty years time half the population over
five would still lack even optional use of a car for getting
about.

Dr Hillman revealed the curious way that planners
valued different people's time for cost-benefit studies: 'Bus
users' travel time is valued at half that of car users, and
pedestrians at half that of vehicle occupants. Children's
time is valued at a third that of adults, whilst the latter's
working time is given six times the value of their non-
working time,' he said. Moreover, the Department of the
Environment had even told local councils not to include
children below secondary school age in traffic counts to
establish the need for pedestrian crossings.

It is apparent that the planners have fallen into the trap
of treating the household as one unit that somehow moves
around in a body, rather than people who each want independent movement once they reach the age of five.
Studies in London show that half the trips that people make
are on foot – and they are not made simply by the lame and
aged, but by active people of all ages and incomes who like
to move around on their own or with people from other
households. Once the requirements of each group of people
are studied, the shortcomings of private road transport
show up clearly and the need for planners to adopt

people as their criterion, rather than cars, become apparent.

Let us take a look at five different groups of people to identify their travel needs and see how they fare in today's car-oriented environment:

Children: In the UK there are 4.8 million pre-school children under five and 6 million primary school children aged 5 to 11. Of all groups the under-fives have the least urge for independent travel, but traffic nevertheless is very much part of their lives. From the time they can toddle they are taught to live in fear of it. Older children however must be able to move around independently if they are to grow up happily, for they are highly exploratory and must learn to grow away from dependence on adults – to be less part of the household unit. In the car society they are restricted: buses are infrequent or non-existent, cycling is dangerous and because of accident risks parents are reluctant to let them go out alone.

Adolescents: 4.7 million of the population are aged 12 to 17 and they spend most of their leisure time away from parents for this is the age of self-assertion and first sexual encounters. They also need to travel independently to and from school. However their leisure is restricted by poor public transport, and from the age of 14 by cost when they must pay full fare. They resent being driven around by parents; they would like to enjoy cycling but now it is dangerous and unpleasant. They fare badly.

Adults of working age: For most of their journeys they need the same independence as other groups. Only the two-car household fares well, for even in the one-car family the housewife is without private transport most of the time. But half the households in the UK have no car, so all their members must depend on public transport for most journeys.

The elderly: old age pensioners number 8.6 million and their happiness rests largely on their ability to get out and about. Loneliness and uselessness haunt most old people, and their plight is aggravated by bereavement and the distance they are from the young couples and their grand-children. Nowadays it is hard for them to keep up the *informality* of their visits to young relatives and so they tend to move about less and less. They seek to remain independent as long as possible and those who do have cars often drive long after their skill is impaired.

The Disabled: no one is sure, but they number between 1.5 and 3 million and their great need is to be integrated into the community. With travel needs like everyone else's, plus hospital visits, they find public transport awkward, roads are hard to cross, while underpasses and bridges are often impossible. The state-aided invalid tricycle is dangerous and isolated and for all except those who now qualify for a subsidized car, life is bleak.

All the people in these groups have different travel needs and the car can only meet a few of them for part of the time. For the rest of the time they must travel by public transport or on foot. But in the growth-committed society a person on foot is an economic nonentity, for he contributes too little towards the Gross National Product. He cannot compete with the motorist, for the car creates jobs, consumes fuel, generates roads, swells the police force, fills hospitals, stimulates research into surgery and psychiatry and requires action on pollution control and noise prevention. In contrast, the person on foot merely uses up shoe leather, and with a weight measured in pounds rather than tons he is exceedingly inefficient at wearing out pavements: they last too long and this is bad for the pavement industry.

For planners, the word pedestrian has all the wrong connotations: they are poor, old or infirm, physically or mentally handicapped, or else too young to merit serious consideration of their needs. The affluent private sector of the economy has little time for such a collection and in consequence they have few to champion their cause. Their sole official organization is the Pedestrians' Association for Road Safety whose objective is safer roads for all, especially pedestrians. The Association is careful to emphasize that it is not 'anti-car'. Its annual subscription is £2.00, and its membership is around 2,000. It ended 1971 with a deficit, has been forced to curtail expenditure and has called for donations to keep going.

The motorist is rather better looked after. The Automobile Association and the Royal Automobile Club have a combined membership of over 5½ million and a joint income well over £20 million. Along with the British Road Federation, the Society of Motor Manufacturers and Traders, the Road Haulage Association and others, the AA and the RAC have generally managed to put the road users' viewpoint whenever they have been threatened.

People on foot need to take an objective look at themselves. For too long they have accepted that might is right and now too much is ranged against them. The police have now developed a conditioned reflex to keep traffic remorselessly on the move. Yet no law compels them to do so. Along with the public they have become hypnotized by mobility, and as good servants of the public they are simply doing what they believe is expected of them. They design pedestrian bridges and subways as a matter of tradition, certain that pedestrians will obligingly climb the ramps and steps. Cars have rather more horsepower than people, yet they stay on the level while people do the climbing. The engineers' opinion of pedestrians is revealed by the bridges and subways they design, as for example writer Terence Bendixson has observed at the new Shepherd's Bush roundabout in London: '. . . the people who inhabit it are out of sight in hurtling metal boxes or underground in a maze of tunnels. There is no place on the ground for humans when the city is redesigned for motoring . . . In effect the tunnels are people-sewers into which pedestrians are flushed as if they were some kind of urban contagion that must be banished from the townscape with the utmost haste.'

If there is one place where the person on foot deserves consideration, it is the High Street. Here is a forum: mothers with children throng it on weekdays, to be joined by husbands on Saturdays. It is the arena for social contact, the hub of the town and its environs. Yet the High Street in town after town has become a race track for through traffic, scattering the crowds, spattering them with mud, filling the air with noise and fumes. To speed the flow, traffic engineers pull down buildings, narrow pavements, cage people behind railings, send them up and down ramps, and all the time ignoring the one glaring truth that the traffic should no longer be in the High Street at all.

The public highway is allegedly public. Yet by paying a mere £25 a year to register a car, one citizen acquires the right to intimidate another, to create conditions which prevent another crossing it or cycling along it in safety, and to impede the progress of public transport. The person on foot has come to accept this process as inevitable, as an insidious adaptation to a lower quality of life. In a world geared to helping the more mobile move even faster, he has simply become the person who gets in the way.

In February 1972, Richard Marsh declared in a lecture to the Royal Society of Fine Arts that the country's transport should be planned as a whole, taking into account the real cost of factors such as congestion, and treating road and rail on an equal footing for costing. He urged a fundamental re-thinking of transport investment by the nation as a whole. It is not within the scope of this book to devise the National Transport Plan that is so urgently needed – to do so would be presumptuous. It is possible, however, to state certain common-sense principles which emerge from our examination of current problems, and then to illustrate some of them with examples of where solutions have been attempted, proposing suggestions where examples are not available.

In Britain so far, planning has been confined to fragmented attempts to meet conflicting aims: futile efforts to build roads which will cope with projected increases in car numbers, at the same time as equally vain efforts to retain public transport as a viable system despite these increases. The study of the social and environmental problems, which has been covered so far in these pages, exposes as a myth the popular concept of universal mobility achieved through car ownership. It postulates instead a very different, alternative aim: *maximum desirable mobility for all kinds of people* – young and old, rich and poor, car owners and carless. It is a simple aim, but the key word *desirable* needs elaboration, for it is used as a qualification in three ways. The first is environmental: in an overcrowded island such as Britain – second only to Taiwan in population density – there is a limit to the amount of moving about that the natural and urban environments can accept before undue strain occurs and the quality of life deteriorates. The second is economic, for as we have seen, excessive mobility absorbs funds and effort which are required for more basic needs, including improvement of the environment. The third expresses the mobility desires of each individual – how much he needs to travel in order to live a fulfilling life. The alternative aim has an important corollary, which is to make transport systems adapt to the needs of *people* in cities, towns and country, instead of requiring people and the environment to adapt to the needs of transport, as has happened till now.

The effects of pursuing the alternative aim will be far-reaching. To cater for the car-less will mean diverting funds from private to public transport, so that in time public transport will become viable. Then taxpayers' money can be released from subsidizing both systems – public and private – as now, and used instead for the more positive task of improving the urban environment, so that there is less need for people to travel in order to escape from unpleasantness. As part of the ripple effect, suburban sprawl and other encroachments on the countryside will be halted and city hearts revitalized – positive benefits arising from the policy of containing mobility within the absorptive capacity of the environment.

Let us now look at some of the practical ways in which the new policy might be implemented.

As we have seen, in order to cater for the mobility needs of individuals the planners have to stop treating the household as one fictitious unit, in which all members of the family have ready access to a car. The next step is to find a way of diverting resources to meet these separate needs, and this can be achieved by liberally interpreting the recognized principle that 'the polluter must pay'. For this it becomes necessary to legislate so that all transport systems pay their true operating costs. For private road transport these comprise noise, vibration, exhaust pollution, congestion, home loss, accidents and so on, and they include the expense of reducing the effects at source as well as compensation for any residual effects. Private road transport should start paying as soon as possible; but public transport not till later, when it has recovered from the long-standing unfair competition of the car.

The immediate effect will be to make public transport relatively cheaper than private motoring, but experience in several cities has shown that this in itself is not enough. To hasten the switch to buses and trains, the use of cars in town and city centres has to be restricted, and this can be achieved principally by drastically reducing parking facilities; for a car, when there is no place to leave it, rapidly loses its attractions. There are other means too: a ban on commuting by car is one: 'road pricing', explained later, is another. A second effect swift to show itself will be a diminished desire by planners to build urban motorways. With fewer cars on urban roads, congestion will no longer be a major problem and urban motorways will be less in demand. Moreover, with the obligation to reduce their ill effects at source, planners will be forced to bury most of them, and when this heavy cost is further increased by compensation measures, urban motorways will be even more prohibitively expensive than at present.

The needs of individuals are again taken into account when resources are switched to improving the environment. Here the keynote becomes one of planning on a 'human scale': buildings become less obtrusive, and people feel less intimidated; light is let in, tranquillity is restored, and a stroll or a shopping trip is safe and pleasant. The needs of children, mothers with children and the elderly take a high priority, and the townscape gains pedestrian walkways, squares, parks and protection from the weather. Cycling becomes pleasurable, young people have somewhere to play and old people somewhere to 'sit and stare'. The American author and traffic planner, John Burby recently wrote: 'The purpose of transportation is to make living, not moving more pleasant.' Let us take a look at how this can be made to happen.

In Britain the Department of the Environment, which has responsibility for road building plans, has paid too much heed to planners and the motorists' lobby and not enough to the needs of people. When, however, the public has been objectively sampled for its views on motorways versus other priorities, the results have been revealing. In 1970 at the time of the Greater London Council plan the Institute of Community Studies conducted a survey among a random sample of nearly 2,000 Londoners to find out what they thought were the most important social priorities. The choice of building new motorways in London came bottom of the Londoners' list. Almost the only research previously commissioned had been by the overtly pro-car British Roads Federation, and not surprisingly *their* results had come out in favour of the GLC's road plan: 19 per cent for and 9 per cent against. Two factors however negated the relevance of these figures: firstly 45 per cent felt they did not know enough about the plan to comment; secondly only 6 per cent of the sample thought it would cost more than £500 million (the estimated basic cost is in fact over £1,800 million!) The Institute of Community Studies in contrast saw little point in asking people what they thought of motorway proposals in isolation, but attached more relevance to suggesting alternative ways of spending tax-payer's money – *their* money – which would have to be forgone if motorways were built. Of the ten suggested alternative claims for their money, 'giving more help to old people' was top with 66 per cent, and 'building more new homes' came a close second with 55 per cent. Then followed a cluster of priorities, ranging from 33 down to 13 per cent, covering recreation facilities, education, air pollution control, buses, railways, the Underground and reducing noise. Way below all items listed came 'more motorways', with a mere 8 per cent.

If people in Britain were aware of the authorities' misconceived priorities, and of their power to influence politicians, apathy could be translated into action and priorities changed. Signs of change do exist: for example the Public Inquiry into the 2½ mile Westcross section of London's Ringway One Motorway in 1972 attracted some 150 objectors. But for dramatic evidence of awakening concern, we need to turn to North America. During 1971, in Phoenix, Los Angeles, Denver, Boston, Philadelphia and Honolulu (just to name a few) motorways were still projected in urban centres, but every one faced stern opposition from amenity groups testing their newly realized power. One of the most dramatic successes was achieved by the anti-motorway group opposing New York City's projected Hudson River Expressway. The fight had lasted six years and cost millions of dollars, largely because Governor Rockefeller had constantly switched routes to keep it alive. In the end he was forced to concede: 'People's priorities are changing.' In Canada action groups also took heart from the scrapping of Toronto's notorious Spadina Expressway, christened by Marshall McLuhan 'the world's most super colossal car-sophagus' and rendered irrelevant by the city's determination to opt for better public transport.

It was two Canadian planners, Sandy and Blanche van Ginkel, who were commissioned to co-operate with the New York Office of Midtown Planning and Development to alleviate the city's torment, as a response to public clamour for action. They produced a plan, eventually approved by the Mayor in 1972, which would create a continuous pedestrian mall all the way from Central Park, along Broadway to the United Nations Park, close most of Central Park to traffic at all times, reduce parking facilities, plant trees in widened sidewalks on famous Fifth Avenue, and take steps to ease congestion in streets carrying traffic. Midtown New York was originally laid out with wide sidewalks for three and four storey houses, but in becoming the densest commercial and retail area in the world, it has narrowed its sidewalks and forced pedestrians in to the rivers of traffic. The plan aims to reverse the trend. The malls would carry pedestrians and minibuses only; they would be lined with trees, shrubs and flowers, have benches and give people ample space in attractive surroundings. Fountains, sculpture, information kiosks, outdoor goods displays, special street signs and lighting and other 'people-oriented' features are envisaged. It would aim to focus movement to clusters of shops, eating and drinking places, and cultural activities.

In Britain, few cities have advanced much further than the limited concession of isolated pedestrian precincts. However, one city with more advanced ideas is Peterborough, which plans to turn the main streets of its city centre into walkways, with trees, shrubs, flower beds and benches. In Europe the boldest plan is for Vienna, where walkers will reclaim a significant proportion of the inner city. Citizens already freed from the proximity of traffic marvel at the new delights: perfect safety, cleaner air, a new, strolling pace of life and, above all, a quietness where footsteps can be heard again.

Britain missed an unparalleled opportunity to design on a human scale for universal mobility when she embarked on the post-war New Town concept. Regrettably, too many fell, like Milton Keynes, into the trap of providing for the 'freewheeling dynamic and mobile society' (to quote the planners), forgetful of the fact that nearly four fifths of the population are without exclusive use of a car. Most New Towns sprawl wastefully: the grid system on which they are usually designed does not suit a public transport system; they have unsatisfactory accident rates; they are ugly and costly to build. Otherwise they are fundamentally sound . . .

But there is an alternative. A few years ago, one planner, Mayer Hillman, had a vision of a town in which all activities of a thriving communal life would be within easy reach of every citizen – and that would include children. Cars would not be restricted: the town's design would simply render them largely unnecessary except for travel outside its boundaries. Instead of fragmented neighbourhood centres, the town he designed had its main centres of activity ranged along a central spine. On either side was a quarter-mile-wide strip containing the compact residential areas, most local, social and commercial activities and some light industry. Beyond it were schools, playing fields, parks and most of the industry which occupy extensive areas of any new towns.

Access to the spine was along 'ribs' of pedestrian ways, providing alternative open or covered routes. No one would have more than a short walk to either the spine or the schools and other centres of activity beyond. Along the spine was the high speed, frequent and free public transport system operating on an exclusive lane. There were access points every quarter mile at junctions with the pedestrian ways.

Each residential area was different in size and character, arranged around private and public 'arenas' of open space, and most homes were sited on cul-de-sacs to eliminate through traffic. Population densities were planned to be fairly high. Stepped housing, rarely more than four storeys high, gave each dwelling a generous private outdoor terrace: it also had the advantage of providing more spacious accommodation for larger families on the lower floors. The town could grow by adding 'offshoot spines' to the main one, each with its quarter-mile-wide strip either side. Such a town would be easy for everyone to get around in, quiet, safe and visually exciting; in fact, a place designed for people, not machines.

As a perpetrator of social and environmental ill-effects the private car is clear leader, though the lorry qualifies for second place. To relieve the burden imposed on the community a similar transfer of resources is required; a shift from road to rail in freight haulage will begin when road transport is required to pay its true social costs, for then rail freight will become more economically attractive. To speed the process, additional legislation will be required, preceded by careful study into this complex and sensitive area. Using the same criteria of the quality of life and protection of the environment, studies can then be made to secure the following aims: the removal of through traffic from side roads in town and country, and from villages and town and city centres; the transfer of local loads from heavy to light vehicles at urban perimeters; night deliveries to shops and businesses. Studies into alternative transport systems are needed, including greater inland use of containers, now extensively used for air and sea freight.

Consideration must also be given to greater use of Britain's 1,500 miles of navigable rivers and canals. There has been renewed interest in their commercial development in recent years, but with the expenditure of comparatively little money they could carry millions of tons of 'dry' goods and even oil, at the same time providing work for thousands. Canals lack the glamour of technologically intensive transport systems; they offer none of the exhilaration of speed inherent in the others; nor do they promise anyone a quick or vast profit. But they can provide safe, quiet movement of goods with the least environmental upset of all, together with *useful*, as opposed to artificially created employment.

Planners have concentrated on towns to the neglect of the countryside. In consequence the people who live and work there, in villages and on farms, have suffered, along with city and townspeople who seek recreation. They have seen their farmland, forests and national parks eroded by suburban developments, industry, mining, water storage and roadbuilding at an alarming rate. Therefore, along with a National Transport Policy there is an equally urgent need for a Land Use Policy to sort out, within an ecological framework, the conflicting claims of all the countryside's would-be users. Because of the planners' neglect, country dwellers have been rendered second-class citizens in the mobility stakes. With their trains and bus services removed, they are now expected to assume the role of car owners or stay put. If there is a policy, it would seem to be one of *laissez-faire*, but the more equable one of finding a solution to stop the drift from villages and farms to cities, towns and suburbs is clearly preferable.

As we shall see, Britain has a special need to conserve her farmlands; recreation land is also vital for the health and sanity of growing city populations, and for these reasons encroachment needs to be checked. Under the alternative transport policy it should be possible to minimize land loss to suburban sprawl, for the switch from cars to public transport, coupled with revised planning criteria, should lead to more densely populated urban communities. Similarly, since the switch also includes lorries, most of Britain's 2,000 miles of projected motorways and dual carriageways will not be required, and continuing land loss to new roads should slow down markedly. However, cancellation of major road projects need not signify abandonment of towns and villages to the ravages of through traffic: the re-routing of trunk roads to avoid stricken settlements can become a first priority.

From the complex matrix of rural problems a number of other considerations stand out clearly as needing study and remedial measures. These include: loss of hedgerows, especially those flanking country by-roads; loss of amenity by mining and oil prospecting; and the overcrowding and degradation of national parks, beauty spots and national monuments, which will be discussed later.

Britain's roads, with over 62 vehicles for every mile, are the most crowded in the world, according to the British Road Federation. The resultant congestion, originally a product of the urban scene, is now increasingly exported to the countryside, and its cure is closely linked with solving the problems of public transport. The solution lies in two approaches: traffic discouragement, and public transport improvement. Traffic discouragement follows the principle already covered: that it makes more sense to tackle the generation of a nuisance *at source* rather than try to clear up the damage after it has been done. Efforts to ease congestion therefore fall into two broad categories: restriction on cars and lorries, and improved competitiveness of trains and buses. Understandably the problem is most acute at peak hours, and F. V. Webster, of the Road Research Laboratory, has found that if car commuters switched to buses, present bus systems could cope and reduce the average journey time for everyone by up to a third. Some of the present car drivers would have longer journey times by switching to buses, but others, as well as *all* present bus travellers, would enjoy shorter ones. If this happened in Central London for example, the saving in vehicle operating costs and passengers' time would be up to £20 million a year.

Because the erosion of public transport has happened steadily over a number of years, its severity has been hidden and its inevitability rarely questioned. Yet in 1969 the Ministry of Transport revealed that: 'The share of the total passenger mileage by public transport in Britain has declined in ten years from 35 to 16 per cent, while the share by private transport has risen from 45 to 74 per cent:' To reverse such a dramatic trend, equally dramatic measures are needed and the prime measures will revolve round allocating true costs. For example, if private motorists insist on driving in town and city centres where public transport can do a better job, a system of 'road pricing' can be employed to ensure they pay the extra cost they impose on the community. In road pricing, a meter is fixed to each car so that the motorist pays as he drives, and the price rises as he reaches the most congestion-prone stretches. The meter, which would be electronically operated from electrical circuits in the road, is quite practicable, and could replace existing taxation methods. It has one big disadvantage however: it confers the right to drive around towns and city centres on those who can best afford to pay, not on those who most *need* to.

Another way to ease congestion is parking control. Many cities' traffic problems could be solved 'at a stroke' if parking facilities, both private and public, were drastically reduced: the visual intrusion of cars would be reduced and buses would move again. Legislation would be required to limit parking on private land, and it would be unpopular – but so is congestion. The *need* to travel by car would be a prime criterion in granting permission to park, and the socially arguable merits of road pricing would not apply. The Department of the Environment has expressed the view that parking control is, in fact, the only practical means of traffic restraint to ease congestion for the next five years. Despite the evidence against parking in cities, the Greater London Council, in its Development Plan, still envisages an increase of 33,000 parking spaces by the end of the next decade.

Since car commuting is the prime cause of urban congestion, a total or partial ban on the practice has been suggested, while another proposal makes use of the deterrent effect of congestion itself. Just as traffic expands to fill the road space available, so it contracts as roads are made narrower or converted to pedestrian use only. Road *narrowing* has been put forward as a feasible, if controversial, way of keeping cars out.

Until the full effects of 'true costing' for private road transport are felt, a number of restrictions to cars and encouragements to public transport may have to be applied during a transition period. So long as roads are choked by a minority of people in cars, the concept of a 'special track' for the majority in buses is an attractive one. In Reading, where exclusive bus lanes were introduced, passengers numbers rose 20,000 a week and revenue £500, while on one key section travel time fell from thirty to three minutes.

In London experimental exclusive bus lanes are operating for six months during 1972 for the critical Piccadilly one-way stretch, with the buses running *against* the traffic – to the predictably furious opposition of the Royal Automobile Club and local stores. In the US an experimental 12-mile-long exclusive bus lane in southern Washington, gets commuters to town 30 minutes faster than by car, and in less than a year's operation, usage has increased 73 per cent. Even the sacred Highway Trust Fund may now be used to finance such lanes.

Free public transport as a means to woo passengers is a perennial topic, with convincing arguments for and against. However, when put in the context of the environmental crisis – depletion of resources and generation of pollution – no scheme which artificially stimulates travel is acceptable as a permanent attempt at solution. But travel need not be completely free. In 1971, Stockholm successfully wooed some motoring commuters from their cars by introducing season tickets giving holders unlimited use of any form of public transport within the Greater Stockholm region for £4 a month.

In Britain it is just possible that the Government is prepared to grasp the nettle and, as first steps, to compensate for noise from motorways and discriminate more against the private car in favour of public transport. Patrick Jenkin, Financial Secretary to the Treasury, weighing his words carefully before the motor trade in 1971, declared: 'The motor car must be our servant not our master . . . we have an overriding duty to see that it does not destroy the quality of life . . .' Early in 1972 the Government set a precedent by paying 75 per cent towards the cost of acquiring buildings in which life had been made intolerable by the construction of new roads. Although the Department of the Environment declared that the case was 'unique'—24 council flats in the London Borough of Tower Hamlets—it has been described as 'a major breakthrough', and represents a change of heart since the Government refused to pay for rehousing people whose lives had been made equally intolerable by Westway.

Discouragement and restrictions are negative and to some extent temporary solutions; the positive approach is to improve the attractiveness of buses and trains as transport systems. Once again we must turn to America if we are to see evidence of a massive swing to investing in public transport. There a $10 billion ten-year programme is under way to 'save, upgrade and improve' the nation's systems, with special emphasis on 'socially and economically disadvantaged persons'. In the three-year period ending June, 1972 the Government provided some $2 billion. Biggest project of all is the San Fransisco Bay Area Rapid Transit (BART) underground system costing $1.4 billion.

Despite the lure of the car, it has been found that people will ride on trains and buses when the systems are clean, frequent, punctual and priced right. In Philadelphia, for example, an improved rail commuter network gained 40 per cent usage in ten years while still employing old carriages and stations. In Chicago a completely modernized railway gained 34 per cent more custom in less time, even though multi-million-dollar motorways paralleled much of its route. Nevertheless, victory will be dearly bought so long as the American car driver escapes his true costs and, like his British counterpart, can drive and park without restriction in his urban centres.

Bus and rail need the benefits of today's technology to bring yesterday's systems up to date. High speed trains, for example, should be able to play a major role in winning travellers from the roads and the air. As the US runs down its space programme and citizen action groups gain more power, manufacturers – especially those in aero-space – are positioning themselves for new opportunities in public transport. The Department of Transportation has begun a multi-million programme to develop innovative designs and systems. In February, 1972, one company was awarded a contract to build the first TACV (Tracked Air-Cushion Vehicle). At speeds up to 150 mph it will glide without

wheels along a concrete guideway on a thin cushion of air, powered by a 'pollution-free' linear induction electric motor.

America is not the only country anticipating the need to supplement – if not replace – the private car transport system. Now that speed has been recognized as the prime ingredient for selling inter-city travel, the technology which makes speeds of over 200 mph possible is being used in Europe and Japan. In Japan, Hitachi is developing a super-express to supersede the already extra-fast Tokaido Super Express. Speeds of over 220 mph create wheel slippage which demands an entirely new concept such as repelling magnets which 'float' the train at up to 310 mph. In the US Ford has studied ideas for 300 mph 'magnetic levitation' trains, hoping for spin-off for its cars.

In Britain, some £6 million was spent in 1971 on two new surface transport systems: the Tracked Hovercraft, developed by the National Research Development Corporation, and British Rail's Advanced Passenger Train. The 'Hovertrain' needs special tracks costing about £1 million a mile, but the APT makes substantial use of existing tracks and signalling, and therefore appears to be the better bet.

The APT, which has been described as a sort of tracked aircraft, reaches speeds of 125 mph and British Rail hope it will be in service by 1978. It will be easy on fuel: a third of the requirements for a normal train at this speed. At 125 mph British Rail see little problem in mixing normal trains and freight on the same lines, and by 1984, when the APT is scheduled to reach its 155 mph maximum, all normal trains will have been replaced on Inter-City routes. The problem of freight still has to be worked out. There is no query about research and development funds for the APT but the Government may need some convincing on priorities if the money to go into production and operate it swiftly is to be forthcoming. As an interim measure, British Rail plan to operate another train, the High Speed Diesel Train, also capable of 125 mph and due to operate in 1975.

Apart from complex ways of discouraging cars and

lorries and encouraging trains and buses, there are other, simple ways of easing urban congestion. In West Germany, flexible working hours have been introduced to stagger rush hour travel: a scheme which will also improve travelling conditions and reduce costs.

In America citizens have taken to bicycles as a means of avoiding traffic jams and parking difficulties, and beating fare increases. Sales rose by a third in 1971 to eight million and the demand for light, fast, fold-away bicycles has outstripped supply. Commuters drive to city outskirts, then park, take their machines from their car boots and pedal away, guilt-free about air pollution, and doing their bit for the national war against obesity. At present exhaust fumes, noise and traffic dangers deter many who would prefer to cycle or walk more, whether in Britain or America. If these ill effects of the rampant motor vehicle can be cut enough, more people will be able to enjoy once again the pleasure of walking – considered by doctors to be possibly the most beneficial exercise for people of all ages.

To reduce traffic noise, once again effort must be directed at the source. Car and lorry engines *can* be made quieter; all that is needed is an incentive. The recent tightening up of regulations on lorries would be encouraging if it were not likely to be offset by the expected increase in weight limits. The technology is available to cut engine noise, but unless forced by legislation the motorist will not pay for the ensuing improvement in quality of life at the cost of poor performance or higher car purchase and running costs. Engine noise *can* be cut, but vibration and tyre noise are tougher problems requiring far more study than has been applied so far.

Laws exist now to curb noise, but they are not enforced. They should be implemented by roadside checks, paid by motorists and hauliers. Where excess noise cannot be curbed, victims are entitled to compensation, not from general revenue, but out of the receipts from fuel and vehicles taxes. Noise that reaches the roads could be reduced by more considerate design. As noise screens, tree planting and green verges to roads are almost useless; but depressed roads would be a big help – fully submerged roads being the only perfect answer. Double glazing – the familiar standby – is *not* the answer, even though the car protagonists, certain economists and the double glazing business maintain it is: for some reason people like to open their windows on summer evenings and enjoy their gardens. Traffic has no right to imprison a person in his home.

The US does not share Britain's complacency over the dangers of motor vehicle exhaust pollution. New York City proposes to require all fleet vehicles to convert to natural gas by 1974, ban petrol powered vehicles from the central business districts the same year, prohibit street parking in designated areas, and require diesel powered vehicles to reduce nitrogen oxide emissions to 20 per cent of the levels emanating from 1970 models. Almost every State is making similar proposals.

To meet the US Government's 1975 anti-pollution target, the car, chemicals and oil industries have mounted a massive effort in research and development. There are thermal re-actors to render emitted carbon monoxide harmless; catalyst converters to remove oxides of nitrogen, carbon monoxide and hydrocarbons; and exhaust gas recirculation systems to limit the production of nitrogen oxides. The vital catalysts, however, can only work properly with lead-free petrol, so the ability to design engines for 'clean' fuel comes first. If this is successful, petrol to run them is likely to cost 2p a gallon more; and more per trip would be needed.

Alternative solutions range from variation on the standard internal combustion engine, such as the German Wankel rotary engine, claimed to answer most pollution problems, or a gas turbine engine as developed by Dr Noel Penny in Britain, to the revolutionary, long awaited electric car, as promoted by the Electricity Council. The electric car, however, cannot be said to solve pollution problems until electricity generation itself puts its house in order;

the car merely moves the source of pollution from the exhaust pipe to the power station chimney. It is unlikely that the problem of air pollution will ever be fully solved, even though technology reduces it far below today's dangerous levels. So long as any form of transport materially lowers the quality of life and threatens the environment, it should follow the axiom that the polluter must pay.

In any accident which injures car occupants there are two collisions: in the first the car hits an obstacle; in the second the occupants hit the hard interior of the car or, if they are flung out of it, the equally hard ground. Because of this, safety efforts concentrate on passenger restraint, the simplest form of which is the safety belt. A more elaborate way of protecting the driver is the 'air bag', which blows up explosively in front of him on impact, creating an instant cushion. Controversy has raged over the air bag however, because of its harmful side effects – damaged ear drums, spectacles driven into the face, and possible chest damage – and critics of it opt for a heavily padded interior with all control knobs, door and window handles completely recessed. Passenger restraint, however, is only part of the solution: door hinges must be burst-proof; the steering column must collapse on impact; windscreens should not lacerate; seats should be securely anchored to car body; the car itself should withstand front and side impact as much as possible, and roll over without squashing. Ideally the car should be incapable of being driven by a person under the influence of alcohol or other drugs. A device developed by a division of General Motors sets a would-be driver a mental test which he must perform before his car will start. However, since the device would add to car costs, GM stated in 1971 that it would not fix it to its own cars unless compelled by law.

The USA, where Nader-inspired citizen action has been most effective, now leads the world on car safety. A recent Federal regulation compels car makers to provide free standard information on safety to all prospective buyers on request so that they can compare cars on the basis of safety. American enthusiasm has finally spread, and throughout the world there is a spate of activity to design experimental safety vehicles, known as ESVs. British, European and US governments and industries are working together on projects totalling some £5 million – an impressive figure, yet still a minute part of the car industries' multi-billion turnover. Alongside the ESV work is NATO's Road Safety Pilot Study, with Canada concerned with alcohol and driving safety, the Netherlands with accident investigation, Italy on emergency medical aid, France on road hazard correction, West Germany on motor vehicle inspection and Belgium on pedestrian safety.

Road improvements can be an important factor in reducing accidents. Although general improvements encourage drivers to drive up to the 'risk threshold', selective ones have been shown to reduce accidents. For example, 'staggered' intersections and properly constructed roundabouts are a help, though roundabouts have the disadvantage of taking up too much land; and to reduce speeds in residential streets, especially made 'lumps' in the road surface near street entrances have been found effective in trials. It is to be hoped that current international research will study just which road improvements reduce the accident toll and which merely increase congestion and encourage drivers to drive to safety limits and beyond.

But much more could be achieved quickly without waiting years for research results. Since speed is related to accident rate and severity, speed limits could be lowered immediately and enforced. Once an acceptable annual accident rate was agreed, speed limits could be adjusted over time to maintain it. Other prompt measures could include: more safety devices outside schools; a special traffic corps to relieve the Police; Highway Code enforcement with stricter penalties; psychological tests for drivers; road improvements at black spots, such black spots clearly marked; special accident treatment services, on-the-spot accident investigation *before* removal of vehicles; soft fronts on cars to lessen pedestrian injuries; more driver onus in insurance schemes; better safety propaganda . . . these are just a few ideas which could save lives.

One fact stands out clearly, the present unacceptable accident rate is demonstrably an engineering one, not a moral one. People can be changed a little by education and coercion, but so long as car design neglects safety, so long as traffic increases, so long as road conditions lag behind requirements, and, in towns, cars mingle with pedestrians, continuing maiming and slaughter will remain the routine daily hazard of private road transport.

9 The Crowded Sky

Each year more and more people travel by air, and aircraft become larger, faster and more numerous. Airports eat up acres of valuable land – usually rich, level farming country or high-priced land near cities – and life is made hell for a growing number of people, battered by aircraft noise. As more jets fly higher and faster, a question mark hangs over the stability of environment: we do not yet know the effects of jet trail-pollutants on the weather, on radiation and air temperature. We do know, however, the disease risk of mass air travel, for it is a highly effective agent for transmitting bacteria from one part of the world to another. And we can see already the harm that mass tourism has brought to the Mediterranean, tropical islands and ancient towns and cities. Without air travel such huge migrations could never have happened. Equally apparent is the growing uniformity of architecture, industry, food, clothing, entertainment and customs through the world, replacing the traditional *mores* that kept societies stable and afforded individuals a vital sense of identity.

The past growth of air travel has been astonishing: the number of passengers carried by scheduled airlines trebled between 1960 and 1970, and 1971 was a record year, four per cent up on the previous one. The number of charter flight and package holiday travellers, which is not included in these figures, also rose steeply in the decade; in 1971 a quarter of the people crossing the Atlantic did so on charter tickets; in 1960 less than 300,000 British holidaymakers travelled by air, but by 1970 there were over two million. In the US, where a plane takes off nearly every second of every day, growth in the late sixties reached a staggering 17 per cent a year.

Although 1971 was a record year, growth during it was below average and forecasters were taken by surprise. Nevertheless the industry has predicted renewed growth, leading to an annual increase of up to 14 per cent and a doubling of passengers by 1976. In Europe, charter business is expected to overtake scheduled traffic by 1975 and move some 63 million people in a year. The package tour industry also predicts continuing growth; for Britain the forecast is 20 per cent a year at first, dropping to 11 per cent by 1975 when over 4.8 million British holidaymakers are expected to fly abroad. In the US growth is expected to rebound to a ten per cent annual increase for scheduled airlines.

In the sixties air freight grew phenomenally at about 18 per cent a year. 1971 saw a drop to only three per cent; but, after a few years, renewed growth is predicted, and forecasts are being made that the volume of cargo traffic will double well before the end of the decade.

Air travel has mushroomed, not because the industry is particularly efficient – few modern ventures can boast more bungles – but because it is subsidized at every turn: from developing and building planes, building and running airports; running airlines – even to private flying as the new 'in' sport. All receive handouts from the taxpayer, yet none pay for the insufferable nuisances they create. The plane-makers give birth to one white elephant after another, either alive or stillborn, and then demand from Government and taxpayers still more money to maintain growth. The irrefutable argument is put forward that national defence, employment and exports all depend on them, and so the industry becomes a magnet for subsidies of all kinds. No self-respecting nation dare to be without at least one airline to carry its flag round the world, whether it can afford the luxury or not. The aerospace industry nurtures the most highly developed technostructure of all, and the planemakers are innovators *par excellence*. No self-respecting airline can afford to ignore their newest offering; if its competitors have them, it must follow suit. Once the rows of seats are there, they must be filled, and when seat capacity exceeds demand – as has happened – fares must tumble. For years fares have been doing just this at the scheduled airlines' back door, for charter airlines have been offering seats at silly prices through two eminently sensible devices. The first was the 'affinity group' business. First a group had to have an interest other than travel itself – relatives abroad or, less ethically perhaps, bird-fancying – and then it simply had to fill a plane. It could charge its members whatever it wished, so fares were usually well below half the regular rate. This business, which started with beaten-up, ex-regular airline planes in the 1950s, had grown so large and lucrative that in time the major airlines had no choice but to let even their newest planes be filled this way. The second device was the package tour business. Tour operators were allowed to offer holidays with travel and accommodation for the price of just the air fare, or even less.

These two devices siphoned off passengers from scheduled airline services. At first, booming business masked the effect, but in 1970 came the introduction of the 362-seater Boeing 747s and nothing was quite the same again. By 1971 over 150 had been delivered to airlines and most of them were flying around less than half full, and sometimes with a mere 30 or 40 bewildered passengers in their cavernous interiors. They had been ordered in the sixties, when growth was running at 17 per cent a year and looked like continuing. But when the Jumbo Jets went into service, growth had slowed, and, worse still, costs had continued to rise. So to fill the rows of empty seats the airlines were forced to act. For a while they played with ingenious, sporadic fare-cutting schemes, but eventually agreed on drastically reduced fares for critical routes, notably the critical Transatlantic run.

By now the circle was complete. Technology had created the means to travel; Government had provided the funds, and marketing men had found the formula for filling the capacity so created. Planemakers and airlines could look forward to a period of profitless growth, increasingly dependent on taxpayers, who – throughout the world – would be repaid by a future filled with the roar and bang of ever larger and louder planes.

Air travel affects us all: even if we never fly, we can no more escape from its noise than from the obligation to support it out of our earnings. For these excellent reasons, its subsidies deserve closer study, those of the planemakers most of all.

If America's supersonic transport aircraft had not been scuttled by the environmental lobby, it would have been the first modern aeroplane in the US not to have been developed out of the Pentagon. Early American planes were straight adaptations of military machines with nearly all the research and development underwritten before the first paying passenger fastened his lap strap. The last of that generation was a Boeing, a jet tanker for refuelling strategic planes in mid-air. To convert it, Boeing simply left out the tanks, put in windows and called it the 707. All the engineering was charged to the jet tanker and paid for by American taxpayers.

Modern civilian planes have little in common with military machines, but the planemakers' overheads are still largely borne by military contracts, and they enjoy all the technological spin-off for free. To fill the gap, governments have stepped in, and since then every major plane for the civilian market has been financed by government grants, both in Britain and America. In theory the goverment aid to research and development is recouped by a levy imposed on sales: in practice the full amount is seldom if ever returned; whether on conventional designs or on exotic flights of fancy such as Concorde or hovercraft.

In Britain the aerospace industry has an annual turnover of more than £600 million; its 400 companies employ over 210,000. British taxpayers foot an annual bill for aerospace research and development of £313 million a year of which nearly half is spent on defence. But even this has not been enough to keep the planemakers out of trouble, and the British Aircraft Corporation has been forced to make large-scale redundancies, chiefly because of lack of orders for its One-Eleven jet, delays in firm orders for Concorde and the disengagement from the European Airbus. In comparison with Rolls Royce, however, its troubles were small. When Rolls Royce got into difficulties with its ambitious RB 211 engine for the American Lockheed Tri-star aircraft, it cost the country £195 million to bail the company out. But this was not all: later the Government contributed another £11 million to a different Rolls Royce project: development of the M45H engine for a West German airliner. Meanwhile in the US Lockheed received a massive US Government-underwritten loan to see them through their Tri-star project.

Against subsidies running into millions a mere £4 million a year could be forgotten—if it were not one of the most bizarre subsidies of all. When Boeing brought out their new 727 aircraft, BEA wanted to buy them for its fleet, but the Government insisted on British-made Tridents, even though they were more expensive to operate and the choice would involve a long and costly delay for the airline. The Government got its way, but as the price of victory the taxpayer was burdened with compensating BEA to the tune of £4 million a year.

In the national status race, supersonic travel represents the biggest prize of all. America is out, though only for the time being; Britain and France, with Concorde, have a modest lead over Russia with her TU 144.

Concorde was sold to an unsuspecting public in 1962 when the anticipated total cost was given as a laughable £150 million. The proposition seemed innocuous: Britain and France would be in the vanguard of a new technology which would bring benefit to all. Peter Jay, in *The Times* of December 10th 1971, described what followed as the gentle art of 'bouncing the Treasury'. The bait once taken, the 'bounceur' remorselessly reels in the helpless sponsor, who first learns that costs have risen slightly and benefits may have to be postponed; however, to abandon the project, would be madness now that the initial outlay has been committed, he is told, and the new estimates of costs are sure to be reliable. They are not, of course, but to cancel now would not only wipe out still further costs committed, but would be to admit publicly to a disastrous blunder, with the risk of political embarrassment. Year after year the process is repeated with variations. If confronted by an economist who reminds him that what has already been committed is irrelevant to the question of whether still more should be committed, the 'bounceur' points out that, bygones being bygones, 'the total benefits of the project now show a very good return on the little remaining to be spent'. The secret is never to admit to *outstanding* costs which are out of proportion to the stated benefits. This way the 'bounceur' can lead the Treasury step by step to a total outlay that exceeds all possible benefits several-fold. To turn mounting criticism, four red herrings can be laid across the trail: patriotism; the necessity to follow wherever technical progress leads; unemployment; and the need to avoid offending our French partners.

By the middle of 1972, Concorde's original £150 million had risen to £855 milion, with some £630 million spent to date, £330 million of it contributed by British taxpayers. In 1972 the plane's selling price was finally fixed at the low figure of £13 million apiece, though, according to M. Pierre-Donatien Cot, the Director-General of Air France, by the time it came into service in 1974, this would have risen to £17 million, plus another £6 million of spares – a total of £23 million.

According to the *New Statesman*, at £13 million, Concorde could well finish up costing British and French taxpayers over £1.4 billion, as the following sum shows:

Production costs	£2,200m
Final research & development	£1,000m
Manufacturers' profits	200m
TOTAL	£3,400m
Income on sale of 150 aircraft	£1,950m
LOSS	£1,450m

This loss excludes any financial aid which the British and French Governments are expected to give BOAC and Air France respectively in buying the planes and running them. By then every British and French taxpayer will have been taken for a ride, though only a few first class passengers will benefit. The few hours saved per passenger will go down in history as the most valuable time ever spent. Each passenger will carry an unusually heavy responsibility in ensuring that such a high priced benefit is not frittered away, despite the negating effects of jet-lag; for the taxpayer and the environment will have paid dearly for every second of it.

Governments will deny it and accountants can conceal it, but airlines throughout the world enjoy substantial government subsidies to make them competitive. And so, from developing countries to industrial states like Britain, the taxpayer foots the bill. Sometimes an airline from a small country is unashamed about its status aspirations. Alia, the Royal Jordanian Airline, says in its press publicity: 'We proudly display the crown because we're a Royal Airline . . . and we are proud of our crown. We want to deserve the right to display it.'

In Britain both BOAC and BEA have benefited from generous Government aid at times of trouble. In eight years of operation up to 1964, BOAC had accumulated a substantial loss, but two years later, when it owed the nation nearly £177 million, the Labour Government wrote off £110 million of the debt and saved the airline some £4

million a year interest payments. Moreover, £31 million of
the debt remaining was pegged at a low four per cent.
BEA, because it was profitable, failed to get the same treatment. By 1969 its £230 million debt had become embarrass-
ing, however, so the Air Corporation Bill reduced its capital
liabilities by some £25 million.

Various financial props help British airlines to compete
with British Rail on their domestic routes. Firstly, the
British Airport Authority adjusts its landing fees to favour
domestic services in order to boost home business. On long
international flights, fees are only a tiny proportion of the
cost. On home flights however they are too large a part of
the cost structure, and are consequently reduced. Secondly,
domestic air services are run at a loss so as to act as 'feeders'
for international flights. In doing so they enjoy all the
facilities of terminals and computers set up for international
business, and operate as a marginal activity. During 1971,
BEA expected to lose some £2.75 million on domestic
flights. Price rises granted by the licensing board are
thought unlikely to wipe out the loss because of the combined effects of rising costs and fewer passengers, so
domestic flights will continue to be subsidized.

Out in the cruel world of international competition the
prospect of growth without profit for airlines in the next
few years spells bad news for taxpayers. Key factor is the
crucial North Atlantic route where the air fare war is at
its most bitter. Hitherto, because of under capacity, the
equivalent of 100 planes a day have crossed the Atlantic
empty. To fill them, airlines are sharpening their marketing
knives, and lowering their fares – and almost certainly their
profits. The *Financial Times* neatly summed up the situation
in September 1971: 'The North Atlantic run is too much a
matter of prestige for governments to let it go, and air
travellers will be subsidized by the general taxpayer.'

Until November 1971, all airlines used navigational aids
in Europe free – costs by courtesy of governments. When
this subsidy was removed, return fares rose by up to £1.40.

One of the new 'in sports' of our generation is flying in

small planes, and even to this small, but rapidly growing activity, aid is generously doled out. To fly for fun it is best to run some business which could conceivably justify a company plane, for once the company has bought it, no check is made on hours flown for business or pleasure, but H.M. Government makes generous depreciation allowances against taxation: up to 80 per cent in the first year and the rest of the cost wiped out in two or three years.

The building of a modern international airport is an undertaking of unbelievable magnitude, complexity and expense. A few, such as Heathrow, have been lucky: they have grown each year at a pace which has allowed extensions and modernizing to be paid for out of operating profit. But when a new airport is planned from scratch – such as London's third at Foulness – the taxpayer pays again, and the prospects of seeing his money back – a cool billion at least – are nil.

Some airports run at a profit, others at a loss. Thanks to Heathrow, the British Airports Authority now makes an overall profit but locally owned Liverpool and Birmingham airports are loss-makers. These cities have followed the European practice where municipalities own their airports and it becomes a question of local pride to ensure that the biggest planes can use them. In 1968/9, municipal airports in the UK cost the public £1.6 million—losses incurred even when large government contributions towards their capital expenditure have been excluded.

In the US the Federal Aviation Authority is liberal with aid for airport development. The Federal Aviation Administration in 1971 approved 43 airport planning projects involving $3.6 billion of Federal funds. Airports and airlines also enjoy spin-off in the form of navigational aids and traffic control systems derived from NASA. The Japanese Government has outraged airlines by reversing the precedent: it has proposed that the building of Tokyo's newest airport should be part-paid by the airline landing fees.

On the subject of charges imposed by airports and

governments IATA Director General Hammerskjold, was adamant: '. . . the financial burden must not be put on the consumer via the airlines', in other words, the taxpayer must pay again.

10 The Assaulted Land

FOR the swollen aero-technostructure, the mobility explosion, even without profits is a Beautiful Thing. But for disinterested other parties, living in surroundings impoverished by it, the effect is a lower quality of life – relieved only by snatches of illusory escape. For an aircraft, whether tiny private plane or multi-engined jet, sends a continuous, moving barrage of noise earthward, which subjects all those below its flight path to degrees of annoyance, ranging from mild irritation to extreme discomfort and even mental illness. The modern jet is a technological miracle of wide-screen movies, stereo, personalized music, armchairs, bars and trendy decor, with rear-mounted engines for passenger quiet. The passenger pays nothing for the racket his journey creates, but an army of citizens below are forced to suffer so that a privileged minority can travel fast and satisfy in comfort their new 'mobility imperative'.

Aircraft are equated with noise. It is worst on take-off, a violent frightening roar as huge volumes of gases and air are mixed, burned and expelled to generate the power to make some 150 tons deadweight defy gravity and leave the ground at around 135 mph. It is objectionable on landing, when the screech of the air compressor and turbines take over to throttle back the massive engines. Even if sonic booms continue to be banned over populated districts – and the supersonic lobby has already begun work to remove this safeguard – supersonic planes make more noise on take-off and landing than subsonic ones, and their noise problem has not yet been solved. As planes get bigger and numbers increase, noise will get worse. The new generation of 'quieter' engines, typified by the Rolls Royce RB211 may offer some hope in the long term, but for the next decade or more, in the absence of any incentive to reduce 'noise pollution' at source, most planes will still be powered by today's unacceptable engines.

Nearly a third of the population of the United Kingdom endures varying levels of aircraft noise and nuisance, but stricter international regulations, if introduced, are unlikely to improve their lot. Around Heathrow alone, some four million people are affected. Doctors near airports cannot work properly. A doctor at West Middlesex hospital has warned of the danger to patients because he cannot listen to hearts or lungs, and another doctor on the Greater London Council has said that under the stress of aircraft noise a surgeon or physician could make errors. Even more important, aircraft noise affects mental health. According to a study conducted in 1959, people living in the 'maximum noise area' for Heathrow – a large, densely populated region under the flight path – are more likely to enter a mental hospital than others. A 1969 survey showed that around Gatwick, Britain's fastest growing airport, householders up to ten miles away have found the value of their houses reduced through increasing aircraft noise.

At a conference of Public Health Inspectors in 1971, Geoffrey Holmes, chief inspector for the badly affected district of New Windsor, said that the whine of jet aircraft saturated whole districts, and, recurring at intervals of every one or two minutes, was 'akin to the Chinese water torture'. It has been estimated that the noise costs to the community around Heathrow airport are about £66 millions a year from loss of house values and amenities alone. Mr Holmes said that grants for sound-proofing homes should be up to 100 per cent of their cost, instead of the present 60 per cent to a maximum of £150 for three rooms. 'The scheme', he declared, 'was an abject failure, because it applied only to houses built before 1965, and even with grants was still too expensive for most people.' Under the circumstances only about five per cent of people eligible applied for grants, and most people did not even know of them. But even if 100 per cent grants were available, sound-proofing is no satisfactory alternative to suppression at source: people like to enjoy their gardens and environment in peace.

The Government has made two surveys on aircraft noise, one in 1961 and another in 1967, both around Heathrow. The second survey found that over the years people appeared to have become more aware of noise as a present and potential menace. More people were rating the district where they lived as noisy and most people regarded noise as a great nuisance, likely to get worse. The survey also found that people were more upset by the nearness and loudness of aircraft than by the steady noise of more distant ones. The survey also revealed that a new breed is emerging, 'the imperturbables', who are becoming adapted to the lower quality of life resulting from incessant noise. It also found that articulate, middle-class people were more inclined to protest than working class people but, as Michael McNair Wilson MP commented: '. . . it is difficult to say whether this is because of a servile acceptance that all's for the worst in this worst of all possible worlds or a fatalistic belief that nothing worthwhile can be done to improve things.'

The investigation undertaken by Stephen Plowden's work on noise costs, described in Chapter 4 is equally revealing on aircraft noise. Owner-occupiers interviewed were asked to imagine they were so close to a major airport that they often found conversations interrupted. Sixty-three per cent said they would move if adequately compensated. Some would need an average of just on £2,600 minimum compensation, others just on £4,400. The remaining 37 per cent, who would rather stay and suffer noise than suffer moving, reckoned they would need at least £950 compensation each. Even in a situation where people were a few miles from an airport, so that although conversations were not interrupted they would have to strain to hear, 45 per cent would move with compensation ranging from nearly £1,800 to over £3,600; and the 55 per cent stay-puts would need over £570 each in compensation.

In 1959 the Noise Abatement Society was asked how to stop the nuisance of aircraft noise around Heathrow. The solution they recommended was to move the airport to Foulness. Twelve years later, after at least £1 million had been wasted on the two-and-a-half-year Roskill Commission, the Government announced the site for London's third airport to replace Heathrow. The Roskill Commission had recommended Cublington, but its terms of reference had turned out to be wrong. When they were put right, the site chosen was none other than Foulness!

Behind that bland decision lay a story of intense citizen action which demonstrated the power of people who develop protest muscles. Those who were threatened formed, in 1969, Wing Airport Resistance Association (WARA) with an active committee, 62,000 members and a leading public relations agency hired for £3,500. Total expenditure on the campaign came to about £60,000. The losers, the rival anti-Foulness group, spent £3,000.

The choice of Foulness saved the loss of hundreds of acres of farmland, historic buildings and the enjoyment rights of thousands of inland dwellers, but its suitability is still in question. The aerospace consultant, Harold Caplan, has called the £1 billion project 'a deception' that would probably never come about, but would generate in ten years the same complaints current about Heathrow. And Adam Thomson, chairman of British Caledonian Airways has stressed that, by the time Foulness came into use, between 1980-85, quieter aircraft would have been introduced; but by then its cost might have exceeded that of Concorde. By then it would be too late to avoid paying an unacceptably high price for the consequences of faulty decision.

What has not been accounted for in decisions to build new major airports is the possibility of quieter planes. Both the projected new generation of planes with engines like the RB211 and the revolutionary short and vertical take-off and landing aircraft (STOL and VTOL) could use existing airports without serious side-effects and render extra, distant airports obsolete before they are finished. The problem is not composed solely of cost and distance, as Peter Scott, the naturalist, pointed out when he put in a plea for wildlife around Foulness, where nearly a quarter of the world's population of Brent Geese will be threatened with extinction. He wrote in *The Times*: 'Man cannot go on increasing for ever, and neither can economics expand for ever. Now is the time to start rigorously cutting our coat according to our planet.'

Local and central government face a dilemma: they would like to gain popularity by appeasing the growing number of protesters to airport expansion wherever they are confronted, but to do so can only invite anger from industry and threaten jobs on which their popularity also depends. So they compromise. After restrictions on night flights from Luton Airport had been imposed in 1971, the local citizens' association promptly described them as a fraud, claiming that the changes were a mathematical manipulation, offering no alleviation from noise, merely confirmation that it would get worse. On the last point the airport's director later found himself agreeing. Similar restrictions for Heathrow, due to operate during the summer of 1972, were hailed as a major breakthrough for peace – until the anti-noise lobby read the small print and learned that sufferers would be woken by engine noise each morning at six; that flights would in fact *increase* during evenings and early mornings, and residents in many populated districts would be even worse off.

At the time of the restrictions on night flying a representative of one airline specializing in package holidays complained: 'It is only by using our airliners at this time that we can keep prices to the public down.' The policy that noise sufferers should subsidize holidaymakers was carried a stage further early in 1972 when the Tour Operators' Study Group, whose 22 members carry more than four-fifths of overseas inclusive holiday traffic, launched a campaign for unrestricted night flying at all airports.

So long as an acute housing shortage continues, there will always be people ready to take the place of those for whom the scream of jets is finally too much – those who have moved from their homes on the verges of runways. Desperate people will do anything, even mortgaging themselves to the intolerable. Once in a while a few people win their battle with the machines – as did those in the tiny Surrey village of Lowfield Heath at the edge of Gatwick Airport runway. For years the residents' association had been fighting for a solution to the noise problem: early in 1972 they finally won. The British Airports Authority cannot buy land simply to lessen the noise burden, however much it feels for those who suffer. But land near runways can be attractive to them for building offices and warehouses, and to others—hotels, airline offices and so on. Early in 1972, Surrey County Council gave planning approval for the demolition and different development of Lowfield Heath, even though it lay within the Green Belt. Soon villagers were reported to be receiving offers of £50,000 and £80,000 an acre – more than enough compensation for the disturbance of moving.

Regrettable though it may be that a runway should encroach on a village in a Green Belt, once the airport is there, only one other satisfactory alternative presents itself: bulldoze it and move it somewhere else—if there *is* anyone else who likes the idea of a runway at the bottom of the garden.

Citizen action over the siting of airports is worldwide. In the US a battle similar to that of Foulness has raged over siting New York's third airport. Planners have looked everywhere from swamps in New Jersey to sites on Long Island and further up New York State. Its site if ever built is expected to be 50 to 70 miles away, from Manhattan, perhaps further; although the Federal Aviation Commission is spending $390,000 dollars to study the feasibility of a close-in, off-shore jetport. Nobody wants it on their doorstep, but status is involved. As Transport Commissioner Sidamon-Eristoff put it: 'The Mayor's Office believes it is necessary to maintain New York's leading position as the port of entry.'

In Los Angeles the City Fathers are applying the most extreme and expensive remedy ever to solve the noise problem of their existing airport. They are wrecking 1,994 homes – many in the luxury bracket – on 400 acres near the International Airport in a 200 million dollar clearance programme. A similar scheme is under way near Montreal in Canada, where two villages and scores of scattered homes in attractive farmland will be cleared to make a 70,000 acre 'noise buffer zone' for a new airport. The Rev. George Duquet, of one of the doomed village summed up the feeling of these displaced: 'In their minds, ownership of property is an essential condition of life. Now the people have lost their property . . . there is no more ambition . . . no more aim in their lives.'

In Portland, Oregon, a $105 million plan to expand Portland International Airport has been delayed two years by home-owners whose land would disappear. The same pattern applies in Atlanta, Boston, Minneapolis, St Paul and other US cities.

But nowhere has the protest been more vigorous and bloody than in Japan. In February 1971, farmers and students joined forces to protest against the threat to land needed for Tokyo's second international airport. Hundreds of demonstrators and scores of police were injured in early battles, and later, in September, students beat three policemen to death during renewed fighting. The weapons range from P.R. agencies to bamboo staves: the motives are the same. The enemy is the god Mobility.

When sailors made contact with South Sea Islanders, and explorers first contacted natives in Africa and New Guinea, whole communities died from diseases such as the common cold and measles – mildly inconvenient to immunized Europeans, lethal to natives with no in-built resistance. Conversely when travellers infiltrated Europe from Africa and the East they brought devastation in the form of the plague, smallpox and cholera. Most primitive people have now suffered contact with 'civilization' and, on the whole have resisted Western diseases more successfully than other importations. The new danger flows the other way: exotic strains of viruses and bacteria, possibly strains that survive the use of antibiotics can now be brought to European countries and the US by plane travellers before symptoms are manifested. During the relatively slow travel by ship, this danger did not exist. Holidaymakers too pose a threat, not only to themselves but to others on return. In territories now on the tourist route, dangerous diseases are endemic; local people have built up a resistance; tourists, unless immunized beforehand, have little to none and are seldom warned. Observers have expressed grave fears that more travel, further afield to countries with sanitation and health services overstrained through rising population pressures, will greatly increase the risk of serious epidemics in European countries, including Britain.

Increased disease risk is not the only personal hazard of air travel. There is the problem of 'jet lag', conveniently ignored by the proponents of fast travel. Jet lag is the effect on the mind and body of the time changes experienced in longitudinal travel, especially west-to-east. Medical evidence shows that it imposes strains on the heart, disrupts the hormone balance and causes irrational behaviour. When added to cross-culture shock it can have a serious disorienting effect.

Doctors who have studied the problem have identified that the effect's intensity depends on flight duration, time zones passed and the time of day or night of departure and arrival. Estimates of the time for full recovery vary. One doctor recommends that, for example, passengers from Montreal to London should rest one day, or from London to Sydney two-and-a-half days. Another says that the body takes up to ten days to return to normal temperature, hormone balance and other rhythms. General mental performance may take four or five days to be fully restored. BOAC have introduced a rule that any executive incurring more than a four-hour time change must rest 24 hours on arrival. Most other companies ignore jet lag. The World Bank is reported as saying: 'Our executives are adults and should be able to decide for themselves whether to take a rest or not.' Yet in 1971 an executive of the World Bank committed suicide after a schedule during which he visited 18 places in 23 days, including Yugoslavia, Paris, Germany and Washington.

One of the justifications put up by the technocrats for the massive investment in air travel and the need to endure the resultant harmful side-effects is the time saved in travelling. It is the sole excuse for Concorde. One thing is now clear: much of the time so expensively saved should be spent in recovering . . . doing nothing!

At any one time, some ten million tons of man-made solid pollutants are floating around in the sky. Air pollution is dangerous and costly. Britain suffers some £150 million a year in damage to materials and health alone, despite all measures taken. In the US the bill has been estimated at over $32 billion a year when all factors are included; a 50 per cent reduction would save the country over $2 billion in medical costs alone. Aircraft share the responsibility for the menace along with domestic and industrial chimneys and motor vehicles. At present its share is probably small overall in comparison with other offenders, but the dramatic growth forecast for air travel and the development of supersonic planes indicate increasing cause for concern, especially in the upper atmosphere. For it is in this region that the Earth is protected from the lethal effects of the sun's energy and the precise temperatures necessary for life are kept in balance. Air pollution could drastically alter the temperature of the Earth; it could increase radio-activity; or it could cause other climatic changes.

Prolonged burning of fossil fuels by aircraft, industry, and motor vehicles is increasing the carbon dioxide content of the air. This allows more of the sun's heat to reach the ground, while trapping heat reflected upwards, as in a greenhouse. If the temperature of the oceans rose in consequence, they would begin to release the carbon dioxide normally dissolved in them. This would in turn intensify the greenhouse effect and the Earth would become hotter and hotter.

This possibility is highly speculative; more probable is a build-up of aerosols in the upper air. The pollutants from aircraft and industry, minute solid and liquid particles, reflect the sun's heat and cause the Earth to cool. A build-up at the present rate might create a fall in the mean surface temperature over the world of up to 3.5 degrees centigrade within the next century and eventually trigger another ice age.

Up at the ten-mile altitude, where supersonic planes fly, lies a layer of ozone which prevents radiation from penetrating below. The waste nitrogen gases from these planes might break down ozone in a chain reaction until the protective layer disappeared. Radiation could then penetrate to blind human and animal life and kill the land plants on which life depends. Once begun, the process could continue even if supersonic flights were later banned.

The white trails of conventional jets have also caused misgivings. In excess they might increase the number of nuclei in the atmosphere upon which rainfall depends, and produce unforeseen changes in the weather.

So far the manifestly harmful consequences of air travel have been chiefly noise and loss of land, and these have been overshadowed by the impact of the car. If the explosive growth of air travel is maintained, however, its other effects will become more manifest and dangerous. So far flying has had a good safety record. The fear attached to flying is largely irrational, possible due to a lack of any personal control over one's fate, and the size of the casualty list of any one crash.

Air travel is hazardous on taking off, on landing or in the

crowded air corridors around airports. It is here that the near-misses occur: 5,000 a year in the US where, over busy airports, internal and international jets moving at 170 mph, share the world's most crowded sky with piston-driven planes doing a mere 60 mph. In Britain the number of near misses is still in three figures, though rising steeply – from 63 cases in 1963 to 108 in 1970.

Gordon Hurley, of the British Air Line Pilots Association said, when the 1970 figures were announced: 'The report indicates the trend we have been forecasting for the past two years. The present air traffic control environment is totally unsuited to cope with the number of air traffic movements over Britain.' From 1963 to 1970 airline movements in and out of Britain rose from 495,000 to 706,000 and, although traffic control has coped, a time is envisaged when saturation point will be reached and a stark choice will be presented: either air traffic growth must be halted or a lower safety standard accepted.

In the US between 1965 and 1969, twelve airliners were involved in mid-air collisions over airports. As John Burby has put it: mid-air collisions are just near-misses with all the luck squeezed out. The number of passengers killed throughout the world in a normal year's flying is now around 1,000, but larger planes in increasingly congested conditions could dramatically change the picture. Aircraft of the future will carry up to 1,000 passengers if Boeing stretches the 747 as ultimately planned: a mid-air collision between two such monsters could kill twice as many passengers in *one crash* as all the crashes now kill throughout the world in *one year*. And if the burning wreckage were to land on just one high-rise block of flats, the death toll could rise to thousands.

If man is to live happily with the aircraft, he must free himself from the strait-jacket of its technological exponential. The first step is to unravel the tangle of subsidies which has shifted the burden of costs from the traveller and consigner of freight to the community. The magnitude of this task cannot be overestimated, for, as we have seen, the industry is intimately involved with defence, economic growth, employment, exports and national prestige. As with road transport, new criteria need to be created and the development of air travel included within the framework of a National Transport Plan, guided also by a Land Use Policy.

Let us examine the problem of costs in the context of the air industries' chief nuisances. Noise need not be the tyrant it has become, for the means exist to make aircraft quieter. Early in 1972, Sir Harry Broadhurst, Managing Director of Hawker Siddeley, said: 'The technology for making them quieter is available to us, it's just a question of paying for it. You add to the weight, you cut down the thrust in putting in these devices, and this means less economy for the airline. In the long run this means the fares going up, and everybody is resistant to this sort of thing.' There were enormous pressures from the public to have cheap travel, he stressed, and at a time of worldwide economic decline, no commercial organization would willingly raise its costs. Since the airlines wouldn't volunteer for this development, it would have to be forced on them: then manufacturers in turn would have to be forced to manufacture and develop the means. He thought Government concern for the environment would have to provide the initiative.

If legislation forced the industry to compensate for its ill-effects in cash, the funds for research, development and production of quiet engines would appear like magic. Already some initial steps have been taken: British, West German and Swedish aerospace companies have formed a joint British-based company to develop a short take-off and landing airliner using the Rolls-Royce M45H engine, already under development. However, whether the project ever goes beyond the feasibility stage will depend on development money from the governments concerned, and that will depend on the priorities they attach to protecting the quality of life of their respective citizens. Once again citizen action reveals itself as the catalyst to change priorities; if it fails, then the millions who now suffer aircraft noise can expect it to get worse each year.

For the ultimate in quiet travel, attention is being turned to reviving the airship. It has other advantages: very low fuel consumption; safety – today's airships use inert helium for lifting power; no runways; passenger comfort. Immense problems of size and economical payload exist, but at least one company is taking the idea seriously.

As with all forms of pollution, the primary aim must always be to reduce it at source. The new, quiet engines achieve the more immaculate solution, but airships, VTOL and STOL aircraft, in totally dissimilar ways, produce a similar effect. VTOL and STOL aircraft achieve their aim by lessening the distance over which they fly at low altitude, but they are costly, long-term developments. Another way of reducing noise by the same method already exists, and although only a partial solution, it could nevertheless be put into practice with benefit within two or three years. Proposed in 1971 by Geoffrey Holmes, of Windsor, the scheme would mean that aircraft would approach to land at a steeper angle than usual, six degrees, until up to three miles from the runway, when they would flatten out to a three degree approach. Current practice is three degrees all the way. For people in Kensington and Chelsea, 12 miles from Heathrow, for example, this would mean aircraft at 5,000 feet instead of 2,500 feet, and 63 decibels instead of 78. Gordon Hurley, of the British Air Line Pilots' Association, has called the scheme 'pretty sound' in theory. It has been tested in California and found both safe and effective. The Government, when questioned in the House, evinced little interest in the scheme, making the excuse that other ideas being examined would, in contrast, require no extra airport navigational equipment. Enquiries have shown, however, that extra costs are likely to be of the order of £20,000 – insignificant in the context of air travel where up to 30,000 people are affected by noise for every mile of flight near Heathrow. A more probable objection is consideration for the comfort of passengers.

If noise cannot be quickly and effectively cut at source, remedial action must take place after it has been generated. Here a number of remedies present themselves. The Noise Abatement Society early in 1972 came up with the most drastic: to close all existing airports as soon as possible. The Society urges that their functions should be taken over by a network already planned: of Advanced Passenger Trains, hovertrains and later an overhead magnetic suspension train service. International air traffic would operate from offshore airports, the first of which would be Foulness. The new airports would be placed around the coast so that no intending passenger need be more than half an hour's journey from an international airport. There is more sense in this idea than may be apparent: in 15 years' time over 85 per cent of air traffic in and out of Britain will be international and by then package holiday traffic will equal or excede scheduled international traffic. And holidaymakers from the Midlands and the North would rather catch a plane from their nearest coastal airport than trek to Foulness.

If all this is too radical – if airports cannot be moved from near-by homes, many homes will have to be moved from near-by airports, costs being borne by the industry. For those who do not move, nothing less than 100 per cent double-glazing grants should be provided. The problem of noise is bound up with the problem of airport siting: reduce noise, either by modifying existing types of aircraft or by developing new ones, then less land is required, and both social and environmental impacts are reduced. The cost of effective research to achieve quieter aircraft? A mere £25 million spread over five years, according to Mr F. B. Greatrex, an expert on noise with the Civil Aviation Authority.

Aircraft, as we have seen, add to pollution of the atmosphere, and, as a matter of some urgency should be forced to reduce their contribution. The need for complete world-wide monitoring of pollution levels which could affect the climate was emphasized at the sixth World Meteorological

Congress in Geneva during 1971. Great concern was for shifts in the Earth's critical heat balance caused by increases in man-made carbon dioxide and dust. Until more is learned, the effects on climate must remain speculative. One fact however is clear-cut: when the Concorde venture was given the green light, the possibility of its affecting the stability of the atmosphere was no more taken into account than the possibility that people on the ground might resent its noise. If Concorde is to go into full-scale production much more needs to be known about its environmental effects than has yet been published, and close, continuous monitoring of possible effects will be required. Never again must any aerospace project proceed in which the social or natural environments are put at risk. Stability deserves a higher priority than mobility.

11   Paella and Chips

EACH summer, North Americans and North Europeans by the million climb on board flying boxes to exchange their little boxes by the city for little boxes by the sea. Innocents abroad, they go armed with a simple faith that they will enjoy themselves and feel better afterwards. Some, chiefly North Americans heading for Europe, are armed also with a determined belief in cultural self-improvement—and an equal determination to take their environment with them wherever they go.

Each summer they all pay a two-week homage to Sun, Sea, Sand and Sex. There are other motives too – curiosity, adventurousness, the need for a rest, escape from squalor, keeping up with the Joneses – but it is the unholy quartet that attracts the millions to the magic fringe. From it has grown one of the largest and fastest growing industries in the world.

In the old days, the people in northern climes resented the sea and left it strictly for seafarers. They built their houses with windows facing inland, for the sea was cold, moody and dangerous. Then in the eighteenth century, when medicine had to be unpleasant to do any good, doctors discovered the sea's 'benign properties', and people, even Royalty, took their ailments to it. From these quiet beginnings the holiday cult began, spreading from the people of means to every class, as first the railway and then air travel brought more and more places within reach. Like most man-made growth it has happened exponentially: the Caribbean, once the haunt of traders, swarmed with Miami's overspill; the Mediterranean, hitherto the reserve of poets, painters, invalids and idle rich, suddenly became the playground of Birmingham and Bermondsey. People, who had become resigned to a denial of achievement within a society which extolled it, discovered that for two whole weeks they could live as they would like to live the whole year round. The duller their lives, the greater was the desire for stimulation, and the more desperate was the urge to taste 'the good life' and emulate the lucky ones.

For the conventional tourist on his first few trips the quartet was enough: sun, sea and sand by day and sex by night. But as holidaymakers became more experienced, some sought more in the customs and culture of the host country. Generally, however, contact with the native inhabitants was limited, and the people of the country remained remote and largely misunderstood. For a time the pattern was stable, but then in the sixties came the armies of itinerant youth, bumming around Europe at first, then spreading across North Africa to the East – pseudo hippies and authentic drop-outs alike, sparking local envy of their freedom along with concern for their morals.

For the millions, however, the consuming desire was to lie in the burning sun, to have drinks served by the pool, as in the brochures, and make the beach the focal point. Inland throughout Europe and North Africa there are millions of square miles with sun, scenery and water for swimming where the tourist armies could be absorbed. But curiously enough, only on the beach can the tourist tan without blushing; only there can he acquire the sexy suntan which proves he went abroad; and just for this are the finest coastlines and oldest cultures degraded.

Never before has there been constant, mass migration on such a scale as now. Millions of ordinary people with infinitely varied backgrounds are, for the first time, coming into prolonged contact with each other. This can promote – as perhaps can nothing else – the understanding between nations that can lessen the chance of war. It can generate respect in people of one country for the culture of another;

it can bring swift prosperity to impoverished people; it can
open the eyes of people in host countries where there is
corruption and oppression; it can revitalize art and create
markets for dying crafts – and it can generate funds to preserve palaces, cathedrals and historical monuments. It can
also offer release for the traveller from his own brand of
tedium: the machine-dominated monotony of his own
industrial society. It can offer escape from a poor climate,
restoring the sick and the weary, and bring pleasure to anyone with even a modest income.

In reality, however tourism rarely achieves more than a
few of these benefits, for its power is a two-edged sword,
and in the hands of the businessmen bent on profit and sun-
seekers after fun, it can do untold damage to the host
country. As things now stand, the tourist lured abroad year
after year by subtle advertising contributes little to such
high ideals. He is lucky to see anything more than the
hotel, the pool, gift shops and discotheques, or meet many
inhabitants apart from waiters, guides, taxi drivers and gift
sellers. Regrettably, none of these were there before he
arrived. The people, along with the rest of the tourist
business, are probably importations, if not from another
country, then from another region. The manufactured
scene is a blend of an environment to make him feel at
home and a spurious atmosphere, in keeping with the
country's promoted image, to remind him that he has
arrived. Spending all his time with other tourists, he may
absorb little of the country, but at least the harm he does
to it will be lessened by his isolation; and it may even be
offset by the kind of prosperity he brings. Not so the culture vulture, the tourist who demands everything: in sufficient numbers his influence on a host country can be
devastating. For, as we shall see, in sufficient numbers any
kind of tourist can inflict damage: with the relentless logic
of the 'tragedy of the commons', he is capable of destroying
the people and the places he pays to see.

The oil industry made possible the air industry as an outlet for its surplus oil; the air industry in turn gave birth to mass tourism to solve the problem of surplus seat capacity. Filling seats is the assigned objective of the tourist industry's marketing men, and they have set about it smoothly and methodically. Applying the techniques learned in other fields, they soon saw that the package required a special ingredient: it was there in latent abundance, the dream of every bored and disillusioned consumer in their target market; it was *fantasy*. And they needed a price incentive too, for the 'fourpence off' formula worked elsewhere; they found it in the cheap, subsidized travel that aircraft provided. The formula worked exquisitely, for the Press needed the advertising revenue and entered the conspiracy with enthusiasm; travel writers churned out reviews of resorts and hotels as empty of genuine criticism as a motoring writer's road test, and as close to reality as *The Sound of Music*.

The travel industry responded to the challenge; needy governments in tourist host countries added more incentives, and in time the marketing objectives were achieved. Today, fast modern charter aircraft can fly a holidaymaker for a mere penny a mile, and hoteliers specializing in package holidays can cut mass catering costs and refine techniques with a precision matched only by factory managers and chicken farmers. The statistics speak for themselves. In 1971, 180 million people visited another country, seven per cent more than the year before. Excluding fares they spent nearly £8.5 billion, eleven per cent more than the year before. Some three million Americans come to the Old World, five million Britons go the Continent, and the vast majority of both groups fly. In 1971, four million people came to Britain on holiday, almost a doubling in five years. On present trends Europe alone will have to cope with 360 million tourists a year in ten years' time. Throughout the whole world tourism is booming – expected to double within a decade.

The publicity beamed at prospective British holidaymakers oozes fantasy on every colourful page, but for the ultimate, again, it is necessary to turn to North America. On American soil, the practitioners of fantasy, the Walt Disney Company, have the biggest stake: Disneyland, California came first; later it built Disney World – 172 times bigger, on 27,500 acres in Florida. And a new contender was McCulloch Oil, which created Lake Havasu City from the empty Arizona desert, centred on London Bridge, shipped stone by stone for $77 million. Meanwhile, in the near-by Caribbean playgrounds other practitioners commissioned advertisements such as: '. . . you'll lunch at the "Floating Oasis" in the midst of our huge freshwater pool. Or shop at our In-the-Inn arcade. When night falls . . . you'll enjoy international and tropical cuisine in our elegantly appointed Plantation Room. Later dance to Calypso rhythms, be entertained by international talent in our bewitching Witch's Hideaway or relax in our Hummingbird Lounge'. The tourist need never leave his hotel. But the inland and Caribbean practitioners had a powerful rival in Europe; Europe was the fantasy land of cities built before commerce had made them indistinguishable from each other; before the car and the brand of progress which America invented had dictated their necessary shape. Europe was meaningful.

The prices of holidays by air themselves border on fantasy. British tour operators can offer holidays in Europe for less than seaside holidays in Britain. Typical 1972 prices: £36 for twelve days on the Costa Brava as against £50 for twelve days at a comparable hotel at Bognor Regis. Winter holidays in Majorca have been offered at a mere £10 all found. And for £300, Americans can have a cheaper two-week holiday in Europe than in Miami. For holidays further afield the bargains are boggling: British tour operators in 1972 were offering inclusive holidays to Jamaica, 15 days for £149; to India, 16 days for £232; and South Africa for £172.

Several important facts of life make this magic carpet miracle possible:

The major tour operators are locked in a deadly price

war, aiming at market share and growth. Even though standards of service are strained and profits are reduced, operators are loath to raise prices. The big firms use scientific business methods and the small ones entrepreneurial ingenuity – there are few in between. Promotion expenditure generates demand. Just one major British operator spends £250,000 a year on advertising and promotion. The government tourist offices of 58 countries spend over £22 million each year. The demand so generated allows travel agents, tour operators, airlines and hotels to use mass production methods. Unit cost can be kept low, so too can profit per unit. Tour operators count themselves lucky if they exceed £1 profit per holidaymaker – one per cent on turnover.

Charter airline companies work to a high load factor—an average of at least 90 per cent to a plane – whereas scheduled airlines, obliged to run a service even for one passenger, are lucky to average 50 per cent. When the European air-bus enters the tour circuit, costs per passenger will be cut still further. Aircraft work flat out – up to 5,000 hours a year. For much of the year they are in the air continuously, grounded only for loading, unloading, refuelling and maintenance. In winter, crews still have to be paid. It costs little more to fly than to stay on the ground, so marginal costing methods are used to price the travel component of the package.

Charter airlines have no promotion and 'window dressing' costs – they just fly and make extra money on in-flight duty-free goods. Tour operators can drive hard bargains with charter airline operators that are competing fiercely for business, and who are in the game largely because flying is in their blood. With revenues trimmed to the limit, standards of service sag dangerously – pre-packed in-flight food fails to meet hygiene standards, planes run late, passengers are stranded, tour operators are inflexible over complaints. But the show goes on. Hard bargains are driven with hotel operators, who are forced to be efficient and cut trimmings to the bone. In return they enjoy guaranteed capacity and freedom to sell surplus accommodation at normal inflated rates. In winter they are happy to cut rates still further to keep scarce staff employed all the year round.

Hotels are often owned by tour operators; alternatively they are leased *en bloc* and in the scramble to make money, they are too often opened before they are ready, or are enlarged around their customers' ears.

Finally the package tour industry benefits directly from the air industry's fortuitous cost structure: the subsidies to planemakers, airports and airlines, and the failure to compensate those who suffer from noise – or stop it at source – all of which create the artificially low fare structure upon which the whole business is based. But for the package tour explosion, taxpayers might not be having to bear the cost of London's newest airport at Foulness.

A two-week £50 holiday would break down roughly as: travel agent's commission £5, hotel accommodation £25, travel £15, tour operator £5. The package holiday is a twentieth-century business miracle. In virtually 25 years it has grown from nothing to one of the world's great industries. Its continued growth depends on three factors in the affluent nations: industrial growth, the repetitive, machine-like work that industry demands, and unsatisfactory neighbourhood environments.

The best part of a holiday is looking forward to it, and next best is looking back: the holiday itself is usually a bit of a letdown, though to admit so counts as rare self-criticism. In fact there is little evidence that holidays abroad are good for people. The journey and the change are not always 'as good as a rest'. Cross-cultural shock can have severe repercussions. And the sun, the number one attraction can actually be harmful.

A touring holiday can be gruelling, for each new day brings a fresh cross-culture shock, as the grim faces of Americans on a 'If it's Tuesday, this must be Belgium' tour plainly show. Cross-culture shock and the stress of travel can cause not only diarrhoea, but headache, unexplained fatigue, digestive upsets and loss of weight. Diseases of sanitation to which the traveller is prone are typhoid, para-typhoid, cholera, dysentry, brucellosis and infective hepa-titis. Worms are also a hazard. Insect-borne infections include malaria, filaria, kala-agar, yellow fever and sleeping sickness. None of these risks appear in the glossy brochures – several are killers. Medical authorities blame package holidays and cheap travel for adding to the spread of VD. In 1970, 15 per cent of the new cases of syphilis in the UK were contracted abroad.

Holidaymakers now face an extra risk. The health-giving sea, which in the nineteenth century began the whole trend, has now reversed its role. Now holidaymakers are likely to be bathing in a solution of industrial effluent and their own sewage. The sea can be a major disease hazard. Swimmers around Europe run a high risk of contracting one or more of the nine diseases known to be caused by faecal pollution. According to a 1971 survey Italian resorts are the worst in the Mediterranean with an 18 per cent disease rate, the French Riviera next with 11.1 per cent, and Spanish waters 10.1. On the Atlantic and at resorts in the English Channel, the rate is down to 8 per cent, but off Belgium it rises to 12 per cent. Illness was found to be up to three times more common among bathers than among non-bathers in places with a bad pollution record. The National Research Council's Water Institute has found that all the water around Naples, Sorrento, Capri and Ischia is highly pol-luted, and waters round Venice, Rome and Genoa only slightly less so. In Switzerland police banned bathers from Lake Lugano when an official survey showed that in some places pollution had reached nearly twice the safety limit. The Mediterranean, jewel of inland seas, is filling with sewage and industrial effluent so fast that, on present trends it will be a dead sea, murky and poisonous, within thirty years.

The effect of sun is one of the greatest misconceptions of our time. Exposure to it is not always healthy, on the con-trary, it is potentially dangerous and can be the holidaymaker's undoing. He is right about a suntan looking sexy, but wrong about the health angle. Somewhere along the way a tan became linked with the Great Outdoors and in itself was thought health-producing. It is nothing of the sort, being merely a defence against the effects of danger- ous excess ultra-violet rays present in rays unhindered by pollution. The tan, for which so many suffer at great expense, is just a naturally produced chemical called melanin, which filters the rays and happens to be a fashion- able brown. Too much exposure to the sun before the body has mobilized its defences causes burning which proves the sun's harmful properties. The defences can be given time to rally by the application of an artificial chemical filter, present in most over-priced suntan preparations – a spin-off market, now worth £2.5 million in Britain alone. The sun ages the skin; it may also trigger off skin cancer. It has only two marginally beneficial effects: it can cure two kinds of rare skin infections and it can correct the unlikely possibility of Vitamin D deficiency in the diet.

Yet the sun is the mainspring of the booming tourist industry, the instigator of the Northerners' annual mass migrations, the indirect cause of the disintegration of native cultures and the dereliction of beautiful coastline and sea. Any value from ultra-violet rays could be had safely at home under a sun lamp with minimal environmental damage.

The tourist abroad runs a gauntlet of risks from disease to sunburn. One day the brochures may carry a warning: 'Caution. Holidays abroad can damage your health.'

In 1971 the Holy Synod of the Greek Orthodox Church published a new prayer: 'Lord Jesus Christ, Son of God, have mercy on the cities, the islands and the villages of our Orthodox Fatherland, as well as the Holy monasteries, which are scourged by the worldly touristic ways. Grace us with a solution of this dramatic problem and protect our brethren who are sorely tried by the modernistic spirit of these contemporary western invaders.'

Commenting on the news, *The Times* in its leader said that, after soldiers, tourists had always been the least considerate of visitors. They were a transient population, temporarily floating free of the anchorage their own society provided. 'Modern advertising', the leader went on, 'puts a premium upon the realization abroad of escapist fantasies. Everything tends to diminish, and nothing to elevate, the visitor's sense of responsibility and his respect for the ways of others.' *The Times* pointed out how tourism invaded cultures whose traditions had not prepared them for the shocking impact of monetary values. The explosion of international tourism represented a tragic dilemma and there was no doubt about its destructive consequences, both physical and spiritual.

Harry Chandler, pioneer tour operator, has expressed his view: 'I would say that if someone has lived in a hovel all his life without a bath and only an outdoor lavatory, and he has now got a television set and a car, he has gained; but a sociologist may say he has not gained anything at all, but has sold his soul for a mess of pottage.' How can you measure the quality of life? If a community was poor and isolated, had little greed but knew mutual trust, and was closely knit; and if that community in a few short seasons is changed by a tourist invasion so that exploitation, covetousness and cynicism become the new order, has it progressed or regressed?

No sensible observer would advocate poverty as a way of life, and great care must be taken not to fall into the trap of romanticizing the simple life. Nevertheless it is apparent that in many countries adversity has led to a stable way of life in which it is the norm for people to share and help each other. The first of the invading tourist armies are quick to notice that the people are animated; they laugh a great deal. The children who play around them are often cared for by all the family, and they have more love and attention than many children in the tourist-generating countries who are handed over to the care of strangers at any opportunity. The old, the sick and the mentally dis-

turbed are unhesitatingly cared for by family and neighbours, and it comes as a shock to 'backward' people to
learn that in 'advanced' countries this is not so.

Mutual help and a spontaneous unquestioning enjoyment of life such as this are found in many countries
scheduled for tourist development as a way out of their
economic mess. When development begins, the first
foreigners are openly welcomed by the community as
guests and as liberators from their plight. In time however
the community begins to experience divisions within itself
which were not there before. Older *mores* break down and
the spirit of group responsibility and mutual help crumbles.
As an imposed, Western style education system takes over,
the new phenomenon of a generation gap appears, accentu-
ated as the young people strive to ape the younger tourists.
Before long the people find themselves forced into the ruth-
lessness of a money economy at odds with the original social
and cultural fabric.

For the majority, the advent of the tourist spells much
needed work, but it is work for which they are not
equipped – menial tasks with little dignity, which leave
them unsatisfied. This they undertake, while around them
they watch foreign developers and hoteliers repatriate their
handsome profits. In such a social climate cynicism grows
and spreads. The tourist is seen to be less a human being,
more an object of exploitation; from there it is only a
short step to exploiting each other; and the newly created
diversions within the culture assist the spread. In the new
economy, tradesmen and some suppliers to the new industry do well, but others in the populace resent the inevitably
rising prices; some incomes rise, but most stay close to the
national level. Inflation soon catches up, not only on daily
needs, but on rents, building costs and land. Local stores
find themselves competing with strange supermarkets.
Streets that were once quiet and safe are filled with cars
and mopeds.

Before they are invaded, most local cultures have a pace
of life which is much slower than the tourists know. They

have not seen the virtue in speed. After invasion they find themselves forced to quicken their pace. In the hotels tourists expect the same service they had at home, and the natives who cannot adapt get fired. Those who do adapt then set the standards for the rest, and the old pace of life no longer suffices. Local dances, music, costumes, dishes die, to be replaced by those of the tourist, while local customs soon degenerate into tourist entertainment. In Tunisia the demand to see a wedding outstripped supply, so mock weddings—for a price—were staged for the unsuspecting. Tourism can commercialize anything and turn even a personal ceremony into show business. In many countries places of worship become little more than market places, as ecclesiastical authorities join in exploiting the tourists, encouraging them to look on churches and cathedrals as museums and bazaars.

At a recent seminar on the socio-economic effects of tourism, UNESCO reported that handicrafts could not compete with mass-produced, often imported goods. Outside the boutique, they are discouraged among the local population as being 'backward' or 'native'. To wear hand-woven cloth and local costume becomes socially undesirable; it is contrary to the desired industrialization of the country and so precious skills are lost. Some local crafts survive only because they have a spurious market value, and they are relegated to phony boutiques of international junk. The crafts soon undergo a change: they become curios 'for tourists only' and their functional attributes are replaced by meaningless decoration, carelessly produced. The craftsmen lose pride. In Spain, for example, cheap imitations of fine Toledo metalwork degrade the centuries-old craft of proud artisans. Hastily made curios from any country may have eye-appeal, but after the tourist has returned home he eventually consigns the fading or disintegrating objects to the attic.

Tourists abroad aim to free themselves of the *mores* that inhibit their capacity for enjoyment at home: this is one of the prime motives for travel. Travel can be heady stuff;

some people over-reach themselves and behave badly. In the host countries, the local people see them at their worst; they quickly learn their visitors' cruder needs, assume that these are what most tourists want, and cater for their lowest appetites. The tourists with more balanced outlooks – by far the majority – sense disappointment and make the hasty judgement that most host countries are corrupt and only interested in tourists for their money, and the circle of misunderstanding is then complete. In the *New York Times*, Paul J. C. Friedlander wrote: 'That malaise that affects the travel industry, by making the natives restless under the gaze of tourists and making the tourists feel – often correctly – unwanted, now has a sociological name. It is called "cultural disparity" or "cultural disorientation".'

Tourism is a capital investment which a developing country can amortize quickly. Countries in need recognize its power. Their tourist boards cannot be fastidious about presenting the truth in their brochures. They remain unconcerned if the tourist is misled in the rush to welcome him. Morocco has spent lavishly on a wall in Rabat, high enough to hide from tourists the squalor of the locals. For many countries, the real conditions inside their borders can clearly be bad publicity, so they are forced to select attractive features, however unrepresentative, and gloss over the major features. The cause of mutual understanding receives a setback.

A country's balance of payments can be quickly transformed by tourism but at the grassroots the picture can be different. The new industry invariably has the effect of encouraging development in some suitably endowed areas to the neglect of others. A social imbalance is created and internal dissension grows.

All mankind benefits from tourism when it saves ancient monuments which would otherwise be lost. But many host countries, in their ignorance, neglect their unique treasures of culture and custom and go out of their way instead to offer the visitor the same sights, the same fare that he has at home. When this happens, the stimulus of the unfamiliar and exotic is gone . . . and in time the tourist may go too. Yet already too many national economies are geared to tourism: for example, the hopes of the Caribbean depend perilously on the health of the American economy; the future of Spain lies uneasily in the fortunes of factory workers in remote Britain and West Germany.

No area of the Western world is so rich in historical significance as the Mediterranean, for in Greece our civilization was born. No area in the world has been so ravaged by tourism, the region's biggest, fastest growing industry. A life style which has lasted a thousand years will soon be gone for ever; the sea will have filled with effluents and, before long, tourist and tour operator will be repeating the process elsewhere. Behind the scenes, and increasingly in public view, the fun fair is grinding to a halt. As Julian Pettifer, TV commentator observed: 'In North Africa the Bedouins have left their flocks to shepherd the tourist and the ship of the desert has become a pleasure boat.' Dancers adapt their symbolic traditions to a belly-wiggling strip-tease to give the customers what they expect. Herdsman and dancer caricature their culture for the tourists' fantasy needs and in so doing they strip themselves of dignity and their own cherished identity.

On the tiny Italian island of Ischia in mid-summer, police calculated that 25,000 cars were jamming the island's 20 miles of road; if placed nose to tail, they would have more than filled the roads in both directions. Ambulances were immobilized, and by the time the fire brigade arrived fires were out. No additional cars were permitted for the rest of the 1971 season.

Venice is not only sinking: as a community it is dying. In 20 years a third of its citizens have left, mainly the young and poor, who can find nowhere to live or work in a city converted to hotels to the neglect of housing. It is atrophying into a museum, in a lagoon of tourist sewage and floating garbage.

In the Portugese Algarve, just west of the Mediterranean, 2,000 natives signed a petition asking the authorities to clean up the old Moorish town of Olhao. They could no longer tolerate the noise of night clubs and motor scooters; they finally rebelled against the strangeness of the strangers.

In Greece, where the Church was moved to prayer, the authorities look forward to a growth from two million tourists in 1971 to ten million in 1980. Population of Greece: under nine million. A desperate country takes desperate measures, tempted by the example of Spain, which earns more than £830 million a year from 26 million tourists, a figure still rising by 10 per cent a year.

Two countries have seen the writing on the wall. Communist Yugoslavia has enlisted the United Nations and accepted their advice that other activities should be fostered, in order to avoid a monocultural development. Tunisia intends to limit tourism to within 35 per cent of the country's GNP. Along with Portugal, both countries intend to control strictly the height, size and architecture of hotels and to avoid the ribbon beach development that has ruined much of the coasts of Spain and Italy. Whether they can preserve their unique quality of life is more open to question.

Islands throughout the world have become the target for tourist and industrial development, in tropical and near-tropical latitudes especially. Hawaii is a glaring example of a culture and a natural environment successively pillaged by missionaries, land speculators, businessmen, politicians and tourists. When the pilot of an aircraft approaches Hawaii he has no trouble finding Honolulu. Over the chain of islands there rises a heavy cloud of air pollution, while below in the ocean the blue is lost in a smear of industrial effluent, soil erosion and sewage. It is said that the missionaries went to the Hawaii islands to do good and they did well. From bible-thumping they turned to land deals, and the friendly, unsuspecting natives soon found themselves landless, working on plantations. The original inhabitants were quickly outnumbered by mobile immigrants who, this century, pushed up the population five-fold to 800,000, and each year tourists swell it temporarily by another million. In consequence, sewage plants cannot cope, famous beaches are infected and coral is dying from algae. When the trade winds fail, Los Angeles-type smog descends, generated by one of the densest car populations in the US and aided by aircraft movements at the rate of one nearly every five minutes. The friendly smile of the dollar-hungry Hawaiian natives is now as false as a plastic *lei*.

From other islands come grim reports. In South-East Asia, Bali is experiencing the vanguard of a tourist invasion through its new international airport. In 1971 the island held a seminar on cultural tourism, on the instructions of the Governor, attended by nearly a hundred delegates. The seminar confirmed that an influential group of Balinese was firmly opposed to tourism as it was currently developing because they saw it as a threat to the country's spiritual life. Specially they feared the commercializing of religious ceremonies and trance dances. Delegates also debated other disturbing effects including the inflow of hippies, increased prostitution and the degradation of handicrafts.

Again in South-East Asia according to Ban It Chiu, the Bishop of Singapore and Malaya, his people often felt that they were made into something like a human zoo. Tourists came along to see 'the natives' who were encouraged to go through traditional movements for goggling strangers. Across the Pacific, Polynesian Cook Islanders face a new future with the opening of their new jet-port, and high blood pressure has occurred amongst the inhabitants for the first time.

In the Caribbean, islands fall one by one: in 1971 BOAC advertised St Lucia as one of the region's loveliest islands, 'waiting to be discovered', to which BOAC would fly a tourist direct for £130 return. By 1973 this tiny 'undiscovered' island can now expect 67,000 visitors a year. Its premier has said he recognizes the social friction that occurs when wealthy tourists come up against local inhabitants of humbler means. He hopes to keep down tourist development to a rate the island can absorb, but its poor economic state may force him to speed up the process.

To get a picture of a Caribbean playground, such as the North Coast of Jamaica, E. S. Turner, writing in *Punch*, has suggested a mental exercise: 'Suppose that all the best hotels on the Isle of Wight have been taken over by blacks for the benefit of wealthy black tourists. Assume that the only well paid jobs for white people in these resorts are those of taxi-driver, waiter, chambermaid and beach boy, with perhaps an occasional assistant managership of an hotel. Finally assume that the luckless remainder of the white population are being urged not to get pregnant.'

In the Indian Ocean, the Seychelles Islands, hitherto isolated apart from occasional ships, opened their first jet-port in 1971 and flights were quickly filled with speculators. Opposing political parties there soon found themselves in uneasy alliance, the Right over foreigners taking the spoils; the Left over rising food prices caused by hotels competing for limited supplies.

Even London can no longer absorb the tourist armies without repercussions. In 1971 six million descended on the city and nearly seven million are expected in 1972. What started as a blessing is changing into a curse. The president of the London Tourist Board, Lord Mancroft, surprised a distinguished gathering with an unusually outspoken plea: St Paul's Cathedral, he said, had been built by Wren for the Glory of God, and not for 'Instamatic cameras and choc ice bars'. He expressed concern that the city was reaching the stage where the sheer discomfort of too many tourists ruined the attractiveness of the London which had brought them there. Moreover the tourist was not the only one to grumble. 'We hear about tourism and the balance of payments, but there is such a thing as the balance of happiness,' he warned. His warning was echoed later by Sir Desmond Plummer, leader of the Greater London Council. 'The growth of tourism, properly steered, could improve the environment, but now and again we get a little worried.

We are concerned with the well-being of the Londoner – the ratepayer and his family. We are very conscious of the fact that too fast a growth of tourism in London could overstrain the resources and lower standards. A good host does not invite more guests than he is ready to entertain properly.'

The British Tourist Authority spends £1 million a year abroad to attract tourists, three-quarters of whom come to London on a well-trodden path. Each day in the season up to 15,000 throng to the Changing of the Guard – though in fact they see very little of it – and the ceremony has degenerated to 'show business'. In Westminster Abbey, charges have had to be imposed and visitors made to keep moving. Around Piccadilly Circus so many tourists spill into the streets in August that traffic has been halted for long periods. Loudspeakers on Thames pleasure boats have impeded work in the House of Commons. In one of the world's most fair-minded communities it has become common practice to overcharge anyone with a foreign accent. The character of the singular streets has been ruined by a crop of brash hotels, and elsewhere has grown the new threat of 'creeping hotels': profiteering landlords eject residents to make way for overnight tourists.

Officially tourism puts Britain some £45 million a year in credit, but not all the money spent in the country benefits the locals: many new hotels are owned by foreign airlines, and profits leave the country; nearly all hotels are staffed chiefly by short-stay foreigners who promptly remit most of their wages home.

More seriously, the forecast of 15 million visitors a year by 1980 is a major factor in building a new airport at Foulness. The British taxpayer will be subsidizing each tourist who arrives by air, whether at Foulness or not.

Apart from Shakespeare country, known to tour operators as 'the milk run', London bears the brunt of the foreign invaders. The rest of Britain braces itself each summer for a kind of civil war. The Isle of Wight's normal population of 104,000 rises to a transient five million during the course of the summer – one of the biggest concentrations of tourists anywhere. But Devon and Cornwall are the main target for stay-at-home Britons, where the chief currency earners are sickly cream teas and plastic pixies. There the fishing villages are now part of the fantasy industry, the dunes are buried under rows of caravans, and those lanes which have not yet been widened fill up with cars.

The British Tourist Authority's 1971 annual report had an ominous Parkinson undertone of generating growth to fill capacity available. The report said that Britain would need at least ten million visitors a year by 1975 to justify the heavy investment in hotel accommodation. The report did *not* say that the impending hotel surplus was due to the Government's infamous Hotel Development Scheme – a straight subsidy to any developer who began building in time. During its two-and-a-half year-life to April 1971, the scheme ate up £49 million of taxpayers' money, to the delight of the predominantly foreign investors. This subsidy *The Times* later described as perhaps misguided largesse and a cause of unease for London, where some £21 million of the subsidy was estimated to have been spent.

Some of the world-wide dangers have already been recognized. The World Council of Churches has expressed concern at the social strains created in small and unsophisticated communities by an excessive number of tourists. The Council has called for serious research into the problem. A study prepared by the International Union of Official Travel Organizations noted that unless governments recognized the social problems of tourism, together with its effects on health and the environment, resources could be overwhelmed to danger levels chiefly through concentrations of too many tourists in too few places. The study advocated world planning of tourism to cope with future growth.

In a free-for-all struggle for the tourist's purse, however, the prospects of international co-operation seem like part of the fantasy and wish-fulfilment aura characterizing the whole tourist industry.

In an over-populated world, where fuel, land and other resources will run short, freedom of travel over long distances must inevitably become more of a privilege and a luxury, less of an opportunity to be squandered. The International Union of Official Travel Agents has advocated world planning for tourism, but whether it is desirable to assume continuing growth is more debatable. In planning, the aim should be not so much how to stimulate the greatest random growth in the interests of profit, but more how to allocate the opportunity for travel more fairly and advantageously to travellers and hosts. There is nothing inherently 'wrong' in travel; the problem is one of making it bear its true social costs and preventing it from destroying the host country cultures and environments that travellers go to enjoy.

Four closely linked problems can be identified as having the greatest need for study and remedial action: over-crowding of popular tourist-attracting localities; standardization of societies; misconceptions and misunderstandings between tourists and hosts; and over-dependence of poorer host countries on tourism.

In the context of the *Blueprint for Survival* the amount of travel in a new social system would be reduced. The travel industries would be required to bear the costs of resource depletion, pollution and noise, and fares would rise. On the other hand, as neighbourhood environments were improved, as near-by recreational amenities became available and, with less repetitive work, the quality of life improved, so the urge for long distance escapism would diminish. Travel for education, especially for young people, could, and should, be encouraged by judicious subsidies notwithstanding. Even so, overcrowding will still be endemic – though less obtrusive – and certain restrictions can be expected. In some sought-after places, where demand exceeds supply, it may be necessary to charge admission or raise existing charges. To restore atmosphere and tranquillity to places of special historic, cultural or scenic value, it may be possible to 'siphon-off' the sun-sand-sea-sex set to designated pleasure zones. Bare, sun-drenched coastlines with good beaches are still to be found, for example, in Italy south of the Pontine Marshes, parts of the south coast of France, in Spain's south-east coast, in North Africa, America and Australia. Since they have little other value, they could be turned over to the escapists without undue environmental damage. Water and electricity could bring them to life and make possible the trees, gardens, pools and essential night life that holiday-makers seek.

Standardization is a problem of equally daunting proportions, with its roots deep in the ambitions of industrialists. The UNESCO Report quoted earlier, puts one aspect of the problem plainly: 'Mass production and uniformity, following from intensified international economic development may soon deprive tourism of the powerful stimulus represented by the unfamiliar and the exotic'. Not until the governments of host countries fully realize that in their uniqueness their countries have a priceless asset, valuable not only for increasing tourist earnings, but – more importantly – for the very stability of their societies, are they likely to take steps to protect it. UNESCO recommend that local governments should be persuaded to raise the standard of local crafts by setting standards with accreditation, while the tourist-generating countries should help to create export markets for them. In a world of sameness, hand-made articles of genuine tradition can find a ready sale when professionally marketed.

The World Council of Churches stresses the importance of *accurate* information about countries in all publicity material. Relations between tourists and those providing services are singularly important: often these people are all the tourist may meet. The Council urges that there be more concern for employees – less seasonal unemployment and overwork, more training and the provision of status – by industries, labour organizations and government bodies. It also advocates the deliberate provision of the kind of encounters which remove national images, such as 'meet the people' programmes along the lines offered by local agencies in Sweden and Germany. Norwegian Caribbean Lines which runs regular cruises for Americans, is one organization which has made an effort. The company aims to educate tourists on how to learn from the people they meet, how to show them the best of their way of life, not the worst, and how to enjoy themselves without giving offence. Similarly it tries to help the native inhabitants to learn from their visitors, to retain the best in their own culture in face of one that may seem superficially superior and more exciting. On board ship a Jamaican family act as hosts for meetings where tourists can ask questions; friendships are made and fears evaporate. A different family goes on each trip. On arrival, tourists are spared the usual rubbernecking routine. Instead walking tours are arranged; an islander leading each group, so that tourists see a thousand things they would miss by coach or taxi. They eat native food, prepared by villagers at local schools, instead of plastic American hotel food. They enjoy it, and mutual respect and understanding start to grow.

The problem of helping the inhabitants of the host country is more difficult, for he has most to gain, and pradoxically most to lose. For him the tourist is a money-bag first, a human being second. To reverse the order, he too needs educating so that he understands the stranger and loses his fear. He must appreciate that he has something precious in his society, so valuable that the tourist pays to see it. He needs help to understand that the dearly bought, but superficial trappings of the tourist can bring him only fleeting pleasure, that it is not worth losing a cultural heritage – let alone one good friend – to gain a transistor radio.

12 Vanishing Frontiers

THE modern industrial state requires that its citizens should be ready to move from place to place as its needs dictate. Its interest in people is more as functions of production and consumption than as people with 'awkward' human needs.

Every year thousands of workers kiss their families and girl-friends good-bye and leave their homes in Eastern and Southern Europe to work for a season or more in the affluent West. For at home there is neither the work nor the rate of pay they need if they are to accomplish their dreams and plans. One season's solid work in a German car factory and a Greek peasant can add a room or a storey to his house. A similar spell in an English restaurant and a Spanish waiter can be nearer to buying his own bar, and an Italian to marrying the girl he fancies or buying the car he covets.

Meanwhile, all over Europe and America another army of young people is constantly on the move, changing jobs, settling briefly, having a break and then moving on. The process is an accepted phase in the process of growing up – for Australians, Britons and Americans, or any young person from a country affluent and liberated enough to let its restless generation make the break.

Elsewhere, in the multinational companies, executives and their families are playing the grim game of 'musical homes'. For some it is scarcely worth unpacking. Employees working for the giant IBM avow the initials stand for 'I've been moved'. And this trend is no longer confined to the multinationals. Changes in technologies, in government's regional policies, in market movements, all require workers of every kind to uproot themselves and go where the action is. In

England, labour turnover in manufacturing industries is now estimated at 30 to 40 per cent a year. In just one year, over 36 million Americans moved house. To capitalize on the phenomenon at least one American company now specializes in counselling families of executives transferred: 'helping them select the right community and home in a new area is our business'. It claims to know 6,700 key communities and will screen them for homes to match the executive's particular specifications.

The daily movement of commuting also has a marked effect on people and places. The combination creates a society where impermanent values are ranked highest in importance and human relationships are necessarily kept superficial. The city of a modern industrial state typifies the throw-away society, for almost everything is temporary: 90 per cent of an American city is expected to be replaced every 50 years: The architecture is always changing; rising land prices force the demolition of old, spatially wasteful buildings to make way for modular high-rise stereotypes; motorway schemes and road-widening trigger new development projects; institutions disappear in mergers and take-overs; corners shops vanish as chains and supermarkets spread and grow; doctors, teachers, tradespeople, workmates, all come and go, often without warning, often without trace.

In any city, close or deep relationships are possible only with a few people. In one week a citizen will meet more people than a villager would once have met in a year, possibly in a life-time. He has two choices; he must either speed up the normal processes of integration, or else settle for a policy of non-involvement and screen most human contacts to the minimum level necessary to function without undue stress. The strain of such unnatural contact is intensified if neighbours and shopkeepers are constantly on the move, for these are the people who would normally be relied upon to endow a sense of permanence in the shifting city scene.

To lessen the pain of severance, a policy of safe, shallow

relationships becomes the norm. 'Other people' necessarily take on a value based on their usefulness rather than their deeper human qualities. The pervading temporary climate encourages a mood of urgency, in tune with the self-generating bustle of the city. In this atmosphere immediate gratification of needs becomes the primary urge; to bank on the future constitutes a risky investment. When community ties are weak, work for it tends to be half-hearted and spasmodic. What is the point in giving up time for neighbours who move on, or for a community you may have to leave? Why plant a tree that you will never see grow?

Even in the relatively more stable suburbs, continuous movement weakens the social fabric. For the commuter lives a double life: his work may take place up to 50 miles away from home, and yet in each of his life's two centres he must build a network of relationships. He can rarely entirely belong in his home neighbourhood, for his livelihood and security depend on the other centre. The bonds which link him with his neighbours have a powerful rival and are weakened in consequence. Because of this people become nostalgic – they look back on a time when, no matter how harsh and shifting the world 'out there' might be, *home* was always a place of permanence and safety; friends could be relied upon. The home environment needs to be stable and satisfying – a pleasant place for man to live. As Robert Ardrey writes: 'If he is a territorial animal, then to repair his dignity and responsibility as a human being, we should first restore his sense of territorial identity.'

When his territorial imperative is thwarted and his tribe has disintegrated, the town dweller seeks instant gratification and turns to escapism. When these palliatives lose their magic, he abandons hope of change for the better, and, however unconsciously, adapts himself to a lower quality of life.

The problem is to change the direction of urban man's restless activity from aimless and self-destructive outlets to socially beneficial alternatives. If a policy of incentives and

175

directives could divert investment and effort to create a better neighbourhood environment, many problems would begin to shrink to manageable proportions. There is ample scope for improvement, not solely in slum clearance, but in reducing the proportions of the city landscape to a human scale. Colin Buchanan has named some of the elements of a city fit for people: somewhere to stroll and sit; trees for oxygen and shade; escape from noise and bustle; a variety of shape, size and width; corners designed to give a sense of the unexpected; the preservation of whole areas and streets of character, not just cases of old buildings. As we have seen, there is a need for more parks, playgrounds and heated swimming pools; compact, high density living near to the ground instead of high-rise flats and urban sprawl, with easy access to countryside—with trees and hedgerows, not one of which should be uprooted in the name of 'progress'. Within the concept of small communities, as proposed in *The Blueprint*, there is abundant scope for towns designed on the principles proposed by Mayer Hillman on page 113.

If, in addition, working conditions could be changed to reduce the numbers of hours of repetitive, unrewarding work, and reinstate craftmanship and creativity – even at the expense of mass-produced trivia – each individual would experience less need for after-work escapism and stimulation. The combined effects of a *human* environment and *satisfying* work should return to the individual his lost sense of political potency, endow him with a sense of having some place in the world, and bring stability to the society of which he is a part.

Neighbourhood environments *can* be improved: it is just a matter of deciding how, and then altering the course of the river of funds. In New York, Central Park has been cleaned up, made safe to walk in and opened to cyclists, and, as described on page 111, the Van Ginkel plan would take it even further; Moscow City Council is providing an enormous girdle of forest for Sunday strollers and a nature reserve; Newcastle's Town Moor and Everton Park are to be redesigned – and the Town Moor scheme will cost no more than a quarter of a mile of urban motorway. The need for still more roads to accommodate week-end trippers will dwindle, if not disappear, if the problem is tackled at source: for by creating a better town environment, there is less need for escape.

To some, a more static society which produces and consumes less, conjures a boring prospect of weeding flower beds and strolling along endless pedestrian malls. It would not be like that, for, as *The Blueprint* points out, there is ample work to be done in reclaiming, building, and caring for the needy; and when that is done, there lies the rewarding world of aesthetic experience. As Galbraith writes: 'Aesthetic development is beyond the reach of the industrial society and is in conflict with it; therefore 'aesthete' has become one of the terms of disapprobation used by the System, which does not encourage enquiry into the value of production. The conflict can be witnessed in battle between highways and open spaces, between high-speed air travel and tranquillity below. Yet only the state can defend the landscape; only it can rule that some patterns of consumption are inconsistent . . . the state must be more than protective, it must be affirmative,' he stresses. 'There is need for instruction in appreciation and enjoyment of the arts. In architecture and urban and environmental design its role is decisive. Even if the results are sometimes bad, there is no alternative to the state'.

The traditional culture of India is as different from that of Norway as is the traditional culture of Indonesia from that of Morocco. Throughout the world, each ancient culture developed as a response to its environment. It evolved from the raw materials of climate, natural resources, agriculture, industry, craftsmanship, art, religion, politics, legal systems, defences and dominant characteristics of its people. Each culture evolved as a distinctive entity because its isolation preserved its individuality, protecting it from too massive or too sudden change. When the means of protection failed, as in large scale war or mass migration, a culture tended to disappear, either through disintegration or through absorption into a dominant neighbour. Today, infiltrating alien industries and mass migrations of workers are adding to the effects of tourism and robbing many cultures of their differences, substituting the uniformity of Western values.

The material evidence is inescapable: all airports look alike; new buildings everywhere are the same high-rise stereotypes; one motorway or parking lot is identical to another; the plan of a new factory was probably drawn up in New York or Detroit; while the prize-winning architect of a new government building was probably from Western Europe; the power stations may be British and the suburbs are inspired by American glossy magazines; schools are European importations; and beach playgrounds have been developed with foreign capital to foreign specifications.

The furniture and plastic gadgets are the same mass-produced design to be seen in any Western city; TV is everywhere with the same ludicrously dubbed programmes, while radio churns out current pop. Clothes are Carnaby Street; food and drink are international and so too are the problems: drugs, drink, demonstrations, violent crime, traffic jams, pollution, noise, economic growth . . .

The infiltration does not stop at the factors creating the problems – it embraces even the attempts to solve them. The twentieth-century panacea of education is one example. 'Developing' countries are encouraged to adopt Western education systems in the belief that they will help them out of their difficulties. Yet, if such education systems work well in the affluent West – which is itself open to dispute – it is improbable that they will work in a country which cannot hope to achieve affluence in a world whose future includes a chronic shortage of finite material resources.

Similarly, the scientific research and development conducted in the affluent countries, comprising nearly 99 per cent of the world's expenditure, is designed to solve their own problems, not those of poor neighbours. In consequence these countries have stayed poor, even where there has been economic growth. As Professor H. W. Singer of Sussex University has pointed out, this research puts a continual emphasis on replacing labour with machines. Labour forces in developing countries are growing three times faster than in affluent ones, but they have only one twentieth of the investment resources of the rich countries.

His observations are confirmed in the 1971 report of the special ad hoc group of the Organization of Economic Co-operation and Development, which urges that affluent countries should foster indigenous capability in science and technology which is relevant to socio-economic situations in less developed countries.

Each individual culture that has evolved throughout the world has been a long, delicate and searching experiment to find the system most appropriate to each people's history, character, environment and prospects. To impose on any people a universal alien culture, invariably American inspired, is as dangerous as it is impertinent. For as the American author, R. Buckminster Fuller, pointed out, biologists studying the extinction of animal species and anthropologists studying the extinction of human tribes have come up with a common explanation: extinction in both cases was the consequence of overspecialization. But that is not all: to woo the under-developed countries from their long-sustained, non-resource-depleting way of life to the Western materialistic-technological ethic, is undesirable because the Western way is not sustainable. When in the course of time it has died, the people who have adopted it will have lost the knowledge and the skills which they employed in the old life, and they will have to attempt the painful process of learning all over again.

Yet today the multinationals, the air travel and tourist industries with their marketing men are actively imposing their life styles on others in the pursuit of profit. They are the new invaders of inadequately defended national frontiers. Growing nationalism in many countries is a sign of a revolt against global uniformity.

The brotherhood of man is an admirable dream which may even be possible. But it will only be achieved with consideration for the differences between people that have arisen from different backgrounds, and will be perpetuated by differences of climate, geography and resources. Universal culture is not to be confused with universal brotherhood.

When man studies the world he lives in, he is at first amazed by the extraordinary diversity everywhere. Later when he approaches the problem as a scientist he is equally amazed by the similarities. Order turns up in the most unlikely places, and what at first seems to be chaos or casual relationship often proves to be a system obeying quite rigid laws. Unfortunately, as science evolved, it split up into separate disciplines with too little exchange of ideas and information. Physicists, sociologists and anthropologists clung to their labels, and the similarities between the disciplines they studied were largely unrecognized.

Soon after the Second World War, however, a number of observers concentrated on the notion that apparently unconnected fields had much in common and were in fact autonomous systems. Norbert Wiener called the study 'Cybernetics'. Ludwig von Bertalanffy and Anatol Rapoport pioneered work into the study of 'General Systems'. The surprising finding was that molecules, cells, biological organisms, human societies and even business enterprises all had much more in common than had been imagined. This helped to explain why some of the specific, separate scientific disciplines fell short of their expectations. Sociology for example, studies the pathological manifestations of modern society – crime, drug addiction, mental diseases and stress, which are all increasing – but does so as if man were unique. In fact man is governed by the same laws affecting the rest of the ecosphere. Each individual is a natural system; so are nations; so are all mankind.

If human societies are not unique, the way they work cannot be understood except by considering them as natural systems, displaying organization and obeying quite rigid laws common to most other things on earth. Edward Goldsmith, Editor of *The Ecologist*, writes: 'If man has been around for one and a half million years, and only in the last 150 has he become an industrialist, this is the equivalent of no more than two days in the life of a man of 50.' For most of his time, man has developed societies adapted to their environments no less than those of other non-human animals.

And so to learn more about man, we need to study other natural systems from molecules to mammals. All systems must obey certain rules if they are to survive – they all have a basic structure in common. If they do not obey these rules they become unstable and break up. Any system is made up of parts which are in dynamic relationship to each other. The pattern of each system may vary, but the parts are always held together by bonds, and though these bonds may be capable of stretching, there is a limit when they snap and a part breaks off. An example is commuting as a cause of the decay of city centres. As commuting distances increase, many people think of themselves more as belonging to their suburb, less as part of the city, and out of working hours they visit it less and less. If the suburb can itself grow into a new sub-system, they are fortunate. If not, they exist as socially deprived members of society, ever searching for a system to join. Until they find one they tend to withdraw or find temporary relief in makeshift associations with others similarly deprived. Another example is Europe's army of mobile workers. So long as the needs of industry demand that people should be units of production suitable for 'plugging in' as required, the bonds necessary for a stable system cannot be forged. Such people neither contribute to a socially useful system nor gain satisfaction from feeling that they belong to one.

A system cannot acquire the essential quality of stability unless its different parts exist in the correct ratio to each other. The size of each part will be governed by the use that the system and its environment have for it. If any part

grows above its optimum value, it threatens both the system and its own security as part of it. In a predominantly agricultural community, the sudden growth of an established industry to suit the needs of a foreign investor can have disastrously disruptive social consequences, and the survival of the industry can be prejudiced. Similarly the growth of an alien method of education can create an imbalance which will dislodge the system from stability.

Any sudden growth, any unprecedented invasion by force or infiltration, can threaten the system if the change exceeds its capacity to cope – either to adjust to the new growth rate or to absorb the effects of the invasion. Stability is not atrophy: all human societies have a history of change, and must continue to adapt to the inevitably changing environment. Social systems need to be open societies – as open as they dare risk being before their stability is lost. That is the tightrope. Their people should have a lively interest in forging just and fulfilling relationships with other people, both within their own societies and outside them, even at the cost of absolute stability.

The survival of any system depends above all on the relationship that it has with its environment. As a highly complex system, man himself has a wide variety of needs, including a sense of aesthetics. The environment created by the modern industrial state fails to provide for this vital sense. 'He cannot work up any enthusiasm for conserving an environment made up of chaotic complexes of concrete blocks or bleak fields mutilated by pylons, factories and housing estates . . . the inevitable concomitants of economic growth,' Edward Goldsmith writes. Such an environment, created specifically to raise the 'standard of living', sacrifices a society's long-term stability in favour of dubious short-term benefits.

A system is an integral whole. To destroy any of its parts risks total breakdown. When Europeans descended on America, Australia, South Africa and the Pacific Islands, the cultures of the original inhabitants collapsed. In most places they ceased to exist, except as a pathetic reminder of a race destroyed, their crafts and customs now preserved for profit in tourist boutiques. When missionaries and colonial administrators tampered with the delicately adjusted cultural system of a stable 'primitive' society, breakdown of the system usually followed, and the survivors ended up in shanty-towns without territory or hope.

Today the eyes of the modern missionaries of industry and tourism, spreading the gospel of global uniformity, are directed to New Guinea, the last great reservoir of primitive cultural wisdom. There, 700 cultural patterns still survive, each with its own language. The stability of such societies matches that of their relationship with their environment, and helps to explain the stability of the New Guinea environment. If one society experiments and in the process makes a mistake, its effects will be limited. Only the actions seen to have lasting benefit will be adopted by the others. If industry and tourism succeed in subjugating the area into the framework of Western style economics, the survival of the region will be placed in jeopardy.

A system, to survive, must have a degree of complexity. If it is too simple it becomes unstable, less likely to cope with unexpected and disruptive changes. It has been the over-simplifying of 'primitive' societies under Western influence which contributed to their breakdown. Any culture which becomes too dependent on one activity is putting itself at risk. If the dollar catch should ever fail, fishing towns now trawling for tourist dollars may find they have forgotten how to net real fish.

13 Towards Survival

THE year 2,000 is no further ahead of us than the Second
World War is behind us. By then Britain is expected to
have a population of 66 million. Her towns and countryside
will bear little resemblance to today's, not only because of
the extra people around, but also because of the material
effects of unplanned economic growth. For growth at four
per cent each year produces a doubling every seventeen
years. If the economy were to continue to grow at this rate,
then within our children's lifetime Brighton to Birmingham
would be one vast conurbation, and trees and hedges
would disappear from much of the dwindling countryside.
Whole counties would resemble neither town nor country,
but more one great factory farm, dotted with industrial
and housing estates, criss-crossed by power-lines and cut
about by the motorways and other roads needed for the
projected 40 million vehicles. This would be the pattern of
development, not only for Britain, but for all the major
industrial regions: Europe, North America and Japan.

If such development were allowed to occur, it would do
so in defiance of mounting evidence that infinite growth in
a finite world is not sustainable. World population will
double to reach seven billion soon after the year 2,000.
Short of some check such as famine, disease or nuclear war,
this growth is inevitable, for the momentum cannot be
stopped. After this, the next doubling is in doubt, for by
then the resources to sustain it will have been stretched to
the limits or beyond. For the planet Earth is a spaceship,
a closed system, with no inputs except solar energy and no
outputs apart from heat loss and occasional rockets. It can

184

be seen that when we have used up all the Earth's natural resources we cannot order any more stocks. The resources will have been dissipated, and to recover even a small part of them would use up large amounts of the remaining material resources and energy. Moreover to do so would produce considerable waste products, and we have already polluted the planet with too much waste. We should like to dump this waste overboard, but we can no more do that than order more stocks of useful materials.

The key resources are food, raw materials and power, and a question mark hangs over all three. The promised Green Revolution, with its new, high yielding strains of staple crops, depends on the ability of monoculture to survive attack from pests and maintain soil fertility. The dates when key materials can no longer be mined are a source of continuing speculation: one report estimates that lead, gold, platinum and zinc will go by 1985, silver, uranium and tin by 1995 and other key metals within the next 50 years. When reserves have been exhausted, industry must rely on recycling and substitutes. Crude oil may be used up within 30 years; nuclear power, the future hope, has grave problems of radio active waste disposal and thermal pollution; alternative energy sources are speculative.

As we have seen, the world is already divided: overdeveloped countries (ODC's) such as Britain, and underdeveloped countries (UDC's) such as India. The ODC's have slow population growths but high economic growths; and, broadly speaking, they depend on the UDC's for food and raw materials. The UDC's have high population growth rates, but low economic ones. They depend on the ODC's for technology and capital. It is an unstable symbiosis, for, as demonstrated, the gap between rich and poor is growing wider, and as supplies run short it is expected to widen still further. The ODC's can continue to grow economically *only* at the ultimate expense of the UDC's, with all the implications of an élite protecting itself by military strength. In such a situation, plans for continuing economic growth need radical rethinking.

In the past few years a number of scientists and industrialists in many countries have become increasingly concerned about the myth of infinite growth in a finite world, with its implications that the UDCs can somehow catch up. One of those concerned, Dr Aurelio Peccei, vice-chairman of Olivetti, founded an informal organization some four years ago to bring scientists and industrialists together. The organization, which became known as the Club of Rome, aims to influence governments, industrial leaders and trade unions to come to grips with the problem. With the help of the Volkswagen Foundation it has begun a project called 'The Predicament of Mankind' to analyse world trends and learn what changes will be needed to survive. The first phase, published in 1972, is based on a complex computer model at the Massachusetts Institute of Technology, and examines the five basic factors which determine growth: population, agricultural production, natural resources, industrial production and pollution. It makes no predictions, but extrapolates past trends to show what would happen to mankind and his environment if nothing were done, then traces the effects of taking various kinds of action. The model shows that, unless economic and political policies change quickly and dramatically from growth to stability, civilization faces disintegration within a century, preceded by a long period of mounting discord and discomfort.

The problem is to save mankind from himself. For as Dr Peccei has said: 'While a lemming or lion, a spider or seagull knows how to be lemming, a lion, a spider, a seagull, man has not yet learned how to be a man.'

The 'tragedy of the commons' is upon us. Each person, each nation that seeks to gain more for himself only robs his neighbours. In the ensuing overall impoverishment everyone faces ruin.

The indications are growing that man is at the sunset of a golden age. For a brief time his life was lit by the prospect, if not the reality, that the majority of mankind might have enough for their needs and enjoy release from toil. It has not quite worked out that way, and now we are recognizing that the dream may never be realized. The only beneficiaries have been the clever, the fortunate and the greedy, and they prosper because technology, which was to have been the key, was applied almost exclusively to the processes of extraction, production and transport. The other half of the task, conservation and coping with waste, was virtually ignored.

It may not be too late to salvage something from the mess of the past to build a future. If so, it will be a very different kind of future from the scenario of exponential growth. This is becoming clear from the efforts of a growing number of scientists and others, shaking themselves free from the constraints of conventional wisdom. As already discussed, in 1972, a diagnosis of the environmental crisis and proposals for its solution were published in *The Ecologist*, a new magazine, hitherto unknown and largely unrecognized. The 22-page document was the work of five people: Edward Goldsmith, editor of *The Ecologist*; Robert Allen, deputy editor; Michael Allaby, editor of *Span*, journal of The Soil Association; Dr John Davoll, director of The Conservation Society; and Sam Lawrence, its secretary. They called their manifesto the *Blueprint for Survival*. It was fully supported by thirty-two distinguished scientists, including five Fellows of the Royal Society, three Professors of Biology, two of Genetics, one of Food Science, one of Medicine, one of Economics and one of Public Administration. The *Blueprint* also launched the Movement for Survival with the aim of influencing governments into taking measures most likely to lead to the stabilization and survival of society. It aimed to obtain maximum electoral support for candidates willing to commit themselves to the politics of *Blueprint*.

In a climate of opinion made apathetic, if not hostile, by an avalanche of doomsday prophecies, *Blueprint* might only have achieved a feeding of egos already committed; but, instead, it made both the front page and First Leader of

The Times, enjoyed excellent coverage on inside pages of other newspapers, and set off a stream of controversy. After it had been attacked by the editor of *Nature*, 187 scientists professionally concerned with ecology wrote to *The Times* welcoming *Blueprint* as a major contribution 'likely to be a turning point in the development of public concern over the ecological crisis'. As with the other scientists, the 187 signatories were not prepared to endorse every detail of the document, but they agreed on a number of major points: stabilization of world population; a Government population policy for Britain, conservation and recycling of resources; and the transition to industrial and agricultural techniques which would not threaten the stability of the environment on which man's well-being and survival depend.

In the *Sunday Times*, Lewis Chester wrote of *Blueprint*: 'For those who, like myself, have regarded environmental considerations as a respectable but not particularly arresting type of cosmetic surgery on Industrial Society, it is mind blowing. After reading it nothing seems quite the same any more'. Later 2,000 students at Manchester University signed it; every department of the British Government discussed it, and the document was translated into all West European languages and Japanese as a prelude to worldwide distribution and publication as a book.

The *Blueprint's* remedies were far reaching: they included proposals such as: *economic growth*, Britain and all other ODC's should try actively to reduce the Gross National Product; *population*, because of her vulnerability as a food importer, Britain should try to reduce population to 30 million, the level at which she can feed herself; *roads*, Britain should stop building roads and redeploy labour to restoring closed railway routes and reclaiming canals, while road and rail public transport should be developed; *resource depletion*, all usage of non-renewable raw materials, including fuel, should be subjected to punitive taxation; *pollution*, those who cause it should pay for preventing it; *recycling*, a company which, in the long term, cannot recycle its waste products to make them socially useful should be taxed out of business; *the Green Revolution* should be halted; *decentralization*, establish small, basically self-suffic-ient communities to create community feeling and global awareness rather than nationalism.

The basis for *Blueprint's* remedies is four conditions which are necessary to establish a stable society: least dis-ruption of ecological processes; greatest possible conserva-tion of materials and energy; population equilibrium; and a social system in which people enjoy, rather than feel re-stricted by, the first three conditions. In any discussion on how the problems of excessive mobility might be solved, it is helpful to see how any proposed solutions are affected by these four conditions.

Minimizing ecological disruption: We depend for sur-vival on the countless ecological processes going on around us. Left alone, these processes always tend towards stability, and the more diverse and complex they are the more stable they become. Any disturbance to them can lead to in-stability: massive interference can spell disaster. If the pro-cesses of industry or agriculture introduce foreign sub-stances into an ecosystem – or even the correct substances in the wrong proportions – and if they are introduced in heavy enough quantities, stability and hence survival are put at risk. To put the environment in jeopardy by the effects of supersonic aircraft, or to continue discharging lead into the atmosphere from vehicle exhausts, for example, would be to ignore these fundamental 'laws'.

Conservation of materials and energy: Conventional economic wisdom places great value on throughput—the passage of raw materials through the System until they emerge as finished products; it is the basis for calculating the cherished Gross National Product. One of the con-ditions of change, in contrast, is a transfer of the economics of flow to one of *stock*. If a tax on raw materials were introduced, it would have the effect of reducing the throughput of raw materials, including fuel, and so achieve the aim of conserving resources and reducing pollution. Its effect on transport industries would be far reaching. All of them squander resources in many ways. They are exceptionally heavy users of oil, not only for propulsion, but as the energy source for the manufacturers of vehicles, aircraft and ships, and the construction of roads, airports and other facilities. The preference for private over public transport adds to the waste, for the energy used in making the cement and steel used in building a motorway is three or four times greater than that required for a railway. The rapid obsolescence of vehicles and aircraft generates an excessive demand for raw materials, and their roads and airports consume not only raw materials, but land increasingly needed for growing food and for recreation. A motorway occupies up to four times as much land as a railway. Suburban sprawl requires more electricity, gas, water and sewage services – and still more roads. As a consumer of materials and energy, excessive mobility produces a pronounced 'ripple effect'. A tax on raw materials would discourage obsolescence and encourage the recycling of materials and components. Since oil is 100 per cent expendable when used as a fuel, it would carry the full tax. An amortization tax, proportional to the estimated life of any product, could also be used to encourage quality and further discourage obsolescence. If land were treated as a finite resource and made subject to tax, its wasteful use – as for motorways and airports – would be reduced; compact town planning would become more popular and private transport within towns and cities would be less popular.

Resource management would serve to protect the world's remaining tracts of wilderness from development by industry, agriculture and tourism. Its function as a regenerator of oxygen and its value as a source of natural genetic material would be preserved.

Population equilibrium: As world population grows, less food will be available for importing countries such as Britain. Such countries have a need to stabilize population and later reduce it to a level at which the country would be self-supporting – about 30 million for Britain on present knowledge. A period of 150 to 200 years is a possible transition time. In this context, plans for Britain's future transport system would need drastic revision. In a non-growth economy and under conditions of a stable population, later reducing, extra roads and airports would be unnecessary.

Creating a new social system: A first step is the improvement of the environment where people live, notably in terms of pollution control and amenities. If a fairer social accounting system than now operates were introduced, it would reveal what new developments society wanted – or did not want. The social costs of any development would then be paid by those who propose or perpetrate it – on the principle that 'the polluter must pay'. The effects of such accounting would be widespread; employment patterns would be affected, but employment could be maintained by diverting labour from production to conservation measures such as recycling and waste control. In this way economic growth would be halted and, as we have seen, new roads would no longer be needed. The labour so released could then be used for such purposes as reviving public transport and reclaiming canals and derelict land.

The keystone of the new social system is decentralization. It would have two aims: to revive community concern and to develop global awareness. Neighbourhoods comprising somewhere around 500 people might be created, these represented in communities of 5,000 in regions of 500,000. These regions would be represented nationally, and the nations would, as now, be represented globally.

In a small community, people can participate and see results; there are fewer 'us and them' problems; and they would be more willing to accept the restraints that would be part of belonging to a stable society than if these were imposed only by some remote government. Within such a community, local industry and agriculture become practicable, and the motives to produce become more rewarding; work is done more for the community than for achieving some distant goal of growth; people are seen to be people, not merely consumers. In a small community the rewards of knowing and being known by a limited number of people should help to create deeper, more lasting relationships than in the contemporary urban scene, and the greater emphasis on human values should help to compensate for the initial hardship of consuming less.

The impact of decentralization on transport and travel would be dramatic. With industry and agriculture localized, commuting distances would shrink, and there would be less need to transport goods between towns. With compact community planning, most travel within it could be on foot or by public transport. For recreation, parks and countryside would be close at hand for those settled outside existing cities and large towns, and in a greatly improved environment, where the human scale of life was re-asserted, the need for long distance escapism would be less.

The new social system and the change it implies will demand as much technological innovation as now, if not more. Only the direction of it will alter: towards providing true social benefits, rather than extending, under its own momentum, the aims of the technostructure. The challenge of living in a way which minimizes ecological disruption and conserves materials and energy will demand all that technology has to offer.

Just one example may help to illustrate. The massive investment in transport has produced a way of life which has been little questioned. It has become accepted that work should take place in centres where people gather: in factories and offices located in towns and cities. To get to work, many people have to commute; once there, many have to travel again to meet people as part of their work.

Over time, roads and railways have spread in a vain attempt to meet the requirement of this convention. All this is the outcome of the technology of the past: the present era has evolved a new way of communicating which could revolutionize working methods and travel, and help to make the *Blueprint* concept of decentralization into a working reality. The new system is telecommunications.

Although now regarded as the poor relation in planning, telecommunications technology could, within a generation or less, enable us to transmit our images, full size, in full colour and three dimensions, over any distance at an acceptable cost. Telecommunications, according to Alex Reid, in *New Society*, could have the same influence in opening up new districts for work and residence as roads and railways have done in the past; and, in contrast, with negligible damage to the environment, and with minimal noise, pollution, and depletion of resources.

Improved telecommunications could ease the pressure on London and other large centres as the essential place for an organization's headquarters, whether government, industry or education – which could then operate effectively with sub-centres scattered around the country. Even more dramatically, the new technology could enable many workers to work within walking distance from home – or even *at home*.

Telecommunication has an advantage which Concorde can never emulate: it travels at the speed of light. Alex Reid writes: 'It might make sense for transport authorities to leave the pursuit of speed to telecommunications . . . and concentrate instead on giving the traveller good working conditions in transit.' If resources are to be switched from road and air travel to more socially beneficial activities, telecommunications is a prime contender. Research is needed into four areas: existing patterns of communications; field trials of forerunners, such as 'Picturephone' and the GPO's 'Confravision'; human behaviour with new systems; and mathematical model-building of ensuing new travel patterns.

Telecommunication is just one example of a switch in resources which the new social system would require. Once the orchestration of change gathers momentum, however whole new fields of endeavour will be revealed. For example in the whole area of transport there is perhaps no greater need than for the efficient movement of food: if a fraction of the technology now devoted to moving materials for industry were switched to the problem of moving food for the hungry, millions more tons would reach them intact and countless lives would be saved.

In general a new social system could lead to a reduction in transport and travel, and an easing of the pressures on the world's tourist host countries. For if enough countries adopted the change to a new social system the whole pattern of international travel would be affected. A general acceptance of change would have even more far-reaching effects; for, with decentralization established as a world-wide concept, the diversity which once existed between communities throughout the world would have the opportunity to return. The new system would be highly relevant to the economies of under-developed countries, and as it spread throughout the world, the dangers accompanying global uniformity should recede.

Professor Rene Dubos recently wrote: 'We must shun uniformity of surroundings as much as absolute conformity of behaviour, and make instead a deliberate effort to create as many diversified environments as possible.' For man's survival the ecological 'law' of diversity is totally relevant.

Much of the world looks to Britain for intellectual and political leadership and Britain could make a massive contribution to environmental sanity. This point was made by Professor Paul Ehrlich, of Stanford University, on a visit to London early in 1972. He stressed that if Britain adopted policies to achieve the long range goal of a population of 30 million, the cause of world population control would be advanced enormously. High on his list of priorities was a restriction on the size and number of cars, which he described as major causes of pollution and as 'resource sinks'.

These changes and others proposed by the *Blueprint for Survival* would amount to a cultural revolution within the framework of democracy. The Movement for Survival, in aiming for political status, envisages a new breed of responsible politicians, freed from old dogmas, in tune with the mood of change and responsive to a concerned electorate. To orchestrate the change from growth to equilibrium, new priorities would be needed, based on social benefit. Much longer planning horizons would be required. The new movement envisages a coalition of organizations concerned with environmental issues, five of which expressed general support at its inception. Not only environmental organizations but many others representing citizen action now have an opportunity to align themselves with the cause of social change. Within the ranks of the electorate, new leaders are already there: all they lack is a common aim. Many of them are to be found among the young, motivated by a deep sense of betrayal.

Charles A. Reich described such young people in *The Greening of America*. He saw them collectively as a spontaneous movement which had already sprouted up, astonishingly and miraculously, out of the stony soil of the corporate state. 'The new level of consciousness which they represent seeks to restore non-material elements of man's existence that were passed by in the rush of material development,' he wrote. 'It seeks to transcend science and technology, to restore them to their proper place as tools of man rather than as the determinants.'

For change to happen, the new leaders will have to overcome apathy as well as hostility. To rouse the public from their present low level of interest in party politics they will need a programme to capture the imagination. The publisher, Maurice Temple-Smith, analysed the cause of political apathy in a series of broadcasts, when he spoke of the Tweedledum-Tweedledee principle. 'Whichever party gets in, and whatever their electoral promises', he said 'all governments seem to have far more in common with each other than with the hopes of the people who elected them.' They were, he believed men with a passionate love of power, who preferred to govern a heavily populated country than face the consequences of over-population, preferred nuclear power stations to national parks, tertiary education to slum school clearance and favoured any grandiose project labelled 'advanced technology' rather than the relief of human misery.

As the authors of *The Blueprint for Survival* point out, the strategy will not succeed without the most careful synchronization and integration, the whole programme extending over many generations. If a smooth transition to the stable society is achieved, children alive today may be able to look forward to a way of life more satisfying than the present one. And the way of life will be sustainable as the present one cannot be, so that the legacy of despair we are about to leave them, may, at the last minute, be changed to one of hope.

The initiative in substituting hope for despair and action for apathy is unlikely to originate from government or industry: for neither is likely to jeopardize today's sales, profits and goals of growth; neither is noteworthy for leading public opinion. There are, however, the beginnings of a third force within the ranks of the people: the groups of concerned and committed citizens bent on action and the righting of wrongs. It is a force which is diverse in age, outlook and aim, and so it is not yet aware of its own power. It includes the young; it embraces those who constitute professional citizenship; and it takes in many established societies and organizations. It has the power to force government and industry to be accountable – to make all those who engage in some activity responsible for the results. At present this is not so; polluting factories are free to dump tons of waste on private land, but if one person throws a brick on another's land he breaks the law. When institutions are forced to become accountable, however, change begins to happen. Citizen action, the new third force, has within its grasp the power to put forward politicians with the vision to create accountable government and bring about change.

In a predicament characterized by exponential growth, every delay only puts the goal further out of reach. This poses a curious dilemma: for, as we have seen, sudden massive change to any system carries with it the risk of disintegration; on the other hand if the change is slow and adaptive, the crisis will overtake us. A way out of the dilemma exists, however: for social disintegration through sudden change is only likely when the change is imposed *from without*; if instead it should grow *from within*, it need pose no such threat. For society to change within the short time that is left, we must hope for a revelation. If each man should discover within himself a concern for all life on Earth, and begin to live accordingly, change too would spread exponentially. There are those in our society who can kindle this awareness; we have need of these people, and with them every means that technological man can muster to spread it across the world.

The change demanded will not be popular. It will be of the order that is demanded – and accepted – in times of war. This is significant, for this *is* war: a worldwide fight to save the air, the land, the oceans, the resources they hold, and all the creatures that inhabit them. Given the will that man can find in war when his home is threatened, we may yet win this Armaggedon. The home we defend is the planet Earth; the enemies are the greed and apathy within each one of us.

Appendix

Readers who wish to become actively involved may find the following list of organizations a useful starting point. Fuller details, including membership subscription, where there is one, will be supplied on request to the addresses shown.

ANCIENT MONUMENTS SOCIETY, 11 Alexander Street, London W.2. Tel: 01-229-5280. Secretary: Dr W. Oddie.

Studies and conserves ancient monuments, historic buildings and fine old craftsmanship.

ANTI-CONCORDE PROJECT, 70 Lytton Avenue, Letchworth, Herts. Tel: 046-26-2081. Secretary: R. Wiggs.

Opposes all supersonic airliners, the sonic boom and the economic and environmental consequences of such aircraft.

ASSOCIATION FOR NEIGHBOURHOOD COUNCILS, 24 Pembridge Gardens, London, W.2. Tel: 01-229-4102. Chairman: D. Chesworth.

Encourages the grassroot democratic conception of neighbourhood councils (otherwise known as urban parish councils) by voluntary effort and statutory provision.

ASSOCIATION FOR THE PRESERVATION OF RURAL SCOTLAND, 39 Castle Street, Edinburgh, EH2 3BH. Tel: 031-225-8391. Secretary: K. Macrae.

Aims to arouse and educate public opinion for the protection of rural scenery and amenities of country towns and villages.

BRITISH ASSOCIATION FOR THE CONTROL OF AIRCRAFT NOISE (BACAN), 30 Fleet Street, London, E.C.4. Tel: 029-34-4200. Secretary: R. C. H. Briggs.

Aims for a steady reduction in aircraft noise.

BRITISH SOCIETY FOR SOCIAL RESPONSIBILITY IN SCIENCE, 70 Great Russell Street, London, W.C.2 Tel: 01-242-8535. General Secretary: D. Dickson.

Aims to alert scientists, engineers and technologists to the social role of their sciences, and create a public alive to the social implications of technological developments, and so able to exercise an informed choice.

Believes that scientists have a responsibility not to carry out research likely to prove harmful.

CIVIC TRUST, 17 Carlton House Terrace, London, SW1Y 5AS. Tel: 01-930-0914. Director: M. Middleton.

Works for higher city planning and design standards; encourages formation of civic and amenity societies and publicizes their activities.

CLEAN AIR COUNCIL FOR ENGLAND AND WALES, Queen Anne Chambers, 28 Broadway, London, SW1H 9NA. Tel: 01-930-4300 Ext. 345. Secretary: G. I. Fuller.

Reviews progress in abating air pollution.

CLEAN AIR COUNCIL FOR SCOTLAND, c/o Scottish Development Department, 21 Hill Street, Edinburgh, EH2 3JY. Tel: 031-226-5208. Secretary: W. M. Robertson.

THE COMMITMENT GROUP, 26 Grosvenor Road, St Albans, Herts. Tel: 56-50910.

Instituted the attempts to block Oxford Street traffic in December 1971; plans continuing direct action to fight the dominance of the car in city centres.

COMMONS, OPEN SPACES AND FOOTPATHS PRESERVATION SOCIETY, 166 Shaftesbury Avenue, London, WC2H 8JH. Tel: 01-836-7220. Secretary: I. Campbell.

Seeks to preserve commons and greens for public use, obtain access to open country and preserve public paths; advises on the law in obtaining these aims.

THE CONSERVATION SOCIETY, 34 Bridge Street, Walton-on-Thames, Surrey. Tel: 98-41793. Director: Dr J. Davoll.

Has as its main aims the stablization of population at the appropriate level and the conservation of Earth's finite resources.

COUNCIL FOR THE PROTECTION OF RURAL ENGLAND, 4 Hobart

Place, London, SW1 WHY. Tel: 01-235-9481. Joint sec-
retaries: M. V. Osmond and A. F. Holford-Walker.

Organizes concerted action to secure the improvement
and protection of the countryside, its towns and villages.
Seeks reports on environmental threats.

COUNCIL FOR THE PROTECTION OF RURAL WALES, Meiford,
Montgomeryshire, SY22 6DA. Tel: Meiford 383. Secretary:
S. R. J. Meade.

DWARFS, 270 Barking Road, London, E.6. Tel: 01-471-
2276.

Corresponds to the non-violent Dutch Kabouters and
Provos; believes in creating alternative ecologically sound
co-operatives to replace existing commercial institutions.

ENVIRONMENTAL CONSORTIUM, 14 William IV Street,
London, WC2N 4DW. Tel: 01-836-0908/9. Press Officer:
G. Hay.

Exists to work on constructive environmental projects
jointly with other voluntary bodies, public bodies or private
enterprises; welcomes approaches from individuals or
groups on specific issues.

FRIENDS OF THE EARTH, 9 Poland Street, London, W1V
3DG. Tel: 01-437-6121.

Works actively to generate responsibility to the environment and make environmental issues the subject of public
debate; selects specific projects which offend the environment.

HOMES BEFORE ROADS, 9 Poland Street, London, W1V
3DG. Tel: 01-437-1984. Director: D. Beecham.

Is a non-party political movement primarily concerned
with the environmental lobby in local politics; willing to
help individuals and groups fighting development and
motorway plans.

INLAND WATERWAYS ASSOCIATION, 114 Regents Park Road,
London, NW1 8UQ. Tel: 01-586-2556 & 2510. Secretary:
J. Dodwell.

Is the only national organization constituted to promote
the restoration, maintenance and development of the navigable rivers and canals in Britain.

LONDON AMENITY AND TRANSPORT ASSOCIATION, 26 Elm Park Mansions, Park Walk, London, S.W.10. Tel: 01-352-5628. Secretary: T. Martin.

Promotes improved transport facilities consistent with the attainment of a more attractive environment for London as a whole.

MOVEMENT FOR SURVIVAL, 73 Kew Green, Richmond, Surrey. Tel: 01-948-0690.

Aims to obtain maximum electoral support for candidates willing to commit themselves to the policies of the Blueprint for Survival.

NATIONAL CONSERVATION CORPS, Zoological Gardens, Regents Park, London, N.W.1. Tel: 01-722-7112. Director: R. Jennings.

Organizes practical work camps in the countryside at weekends and holiday times to improve wildlife habitats and recreation amenities. Open to anyone over sixteen.

NATIONAL COUNCIL ON INLAND TRANSPORT, 396 City Road, London, E.C.1. Tel: 01-837-9145. Secretary: R. Calvert.

Exists to promote a more enlightened transport policy.

NATIONAL SOCIETY FOR CLEAN AIR, 134-137 North Street, Brighton, BN1 1RG, Sussex. Tel: 0273-26313.

Promotes clean air in the United Kingdom by creating an informed public opinion on its importance.

NOISE ABATEMENT SOCIETY, 6 Old Bond Street, London, W.1. Tel: 01-493-5877. Secretary: I. Campbell.

Has as its sole aim the elimination of excessive and unnecessary noise from all sources.

PEDESTRIANS' ASSOCIATION FOR ROAD SAFETY, 161 Shaftesbury Avenue, London, WC2H 8JH. Tel: 01-836-7220. Secretary: I. Campbell.

Safeguards the needs and interests of pedestrians; opposes increased weight limits for heavy goods vehicles.

'Q', 65 Artesian Road, London, W2 5DB. Tel: 01-229-7855. Newsletter Editor: T. Mills.

Has the sole aim of making sure the human race survives: an international body of ordinary people with neither officials nor committee.

RAMBLERS' ASSOCIATION, 1-4 Crawford Mews, York Street, London, W.1. Tel: 01-262-1477. Secretary: C. Hall.

Protects the rights of the public on country paths, works to secure the right of the public to the open country and to preserve the beauty of the country.

TOWN AND COUNTRY PLANNING ASSOCIATION, 17 Carlton House Terrace, London, SW1Y 5AS. Tel: 01-930-8903-5. Director: D. Hall.

Advocates and promotes understanding of planning policies to improve living and working conditions, safeguard countryside and farmland, enhance natural, architectural and cultural amenities and advance economic efficiency.

TRANSPORT REFORM GROUP, The Old Bakehouse, South Newington, Banbury, Oxfordshire. Tel: 029-572-453. Secretary: Mrs M. Chanter.

Aims to press for complete reappraisal of transport policy on the basis of environmental and social needs, and to appear at public hearings until this is achieved.

Bibliography

ARDREY, Robert. 1967: *The Territorial Imperative*. (Collins)

BANHAM, Reyner. 1971: *Los Angeles, The Architecture of Four Ecologies*. (Penguin)

BARR, John. 1970: *Assaults on our Senses*. (Methuen)

BUCHANAN, Colin. 1958: *Mixed Blessing*. (Leonard Hill)

BUCHANAN, Colin. 1969: *Traffic in Towns* (Penguin)

BURBY, John. 1971: *The Great American Motion Sickness*. (Little, Brown: Boston)

DORST, Jean. 1970: *Before Nature Dies*. (Collins)

EHRLICH, Paul R. & HARRIMAN Richard L. 1971: *How to be a survivor*. (Ballantine)

FALK, Richard A. 1971: *This Endangered Planet*. (Random House, New York)

GALBRAITH, John Kenneth. 1958: *The Affluent Society*. (Hamish Hamilton, Penguin)

GALBRAITH, John Kenneth. 1967: *The New Industrial State*. (Andre Deutsch, Penguin)

GLASSER, Ralph. 1967: *The New High Priesthood*. (Macmillan)

GILL, CRISPIN and others. 1967: *The Wreck of the Torrey Canyon*. (David & Charles)

GOLDSMITH, Edward. 1971: *Can Britain Survive?* (Tom Stacey)

GOLDSMITH, Edward and others. 1972: *The Blueprint for Survival*. (Penguin)

LEAVITT, Helen. 1970: *Superhighway—Superhoax*. (Doubleday: New York)

MISHAN, Edward J. 1967: *The Costs of Economic Growth*. (Staples Press, Penguin)

Morris, Desmond. 1969: *The Human Zoo*. (Jonathan Cape, Corgi)

Nader, Ralph. 1965: *Unsafe at any Speed*. (Grossman)

Parry, Meyer. 1971: *Aggression on the Road*. (Tavistock Publications)

Petrow, Richard. 1968: *Black Tide*. (Hodder and Stoughton)

Plowden, William. 1971: *The Motor Car & Politics*. (Bodley Head)

Reich, Charles A. 1971: *The Greening of America*. (Penguin)

Thomson, J. Michael. 1969: *Motorways in London*. (Duckworth)

Toffler, Alvin. 1970: *Future Shock*. (Bodley Head)

Tugendhat, Christopher. 1971: *The Multinationals*. (Eyre & Spottiswood)

Tugendhat, Christopher. 1968: *Oil, The Biggest Business* (Eyre & Spottiswood)

Whitlock, A. F. 1971: *Death on the Road*. (Tavistock)

Science, Growth and Society: a New Perspective. 1971: *Organization of Economic Co-operation and Development*.

Drive, The Ecologist, The Economist, Evening Standard, Financial Times, Fortune, Futures, Guardian, The Listener, New Scientist, New Society, New Statesman, New York Review of Books, New York Times, Observer, Punch, Sunday Times, The Times.

Index

Noise:
aircraft 136-142
traffic 43-47, 121-122

Obsolescence 62, 190
Oil 26, 29-37, 153-154, 190
Organization of Economic Co-operation and Development 179
Over-developed countries 27, 185
Oxford 82

Parking 109, 117
Parkinson's Law 78, 169
Parry, Meyer H. 56
Peccei, Dr Aurelio 186
Pedestrians 60-61, 102-108, 110-113, 125, 176
Pedestrians' Association for Road Safety 105
Penny, Dr Noel 122
Petworth Park 85
Peyton, John 99
Piccard, Professor Jacques 32, 48
Planning blight 83
Plowden, Stephen 46-47, 138
Plummer, Sir Desmond 167
Police 42, 124
Polluter must pay 109, 123, 188
Pollution:
air 13, 30, 43, 47-50, 122-123, 144-145, 149-150
lake 18, 158
land 30-31, 87-88
ocean 31-35, 158
general 16, 24-25, 186, 188, 191, 196
Population 15, 17, 83, 97, 184, 188, 190-191, 194
Project on Corporate Responsibility 66
Public Transport:
buses 97-101, 117
trains 79-80, 91-92, 94-97, 119-120, 149
general 43, 89-94, 109, 116
Punch 167

Quality of life 18, 107, 138, 160, 175

Railways (See Public Transport)
Ramblers' Association 87
Reading 117
Recycling 188
Reich, Charles A. 195
Resources 28, 185-186, 188-190
Road Haulage Association 106
Road Pricing 109, 116-117
Road Research Laboratory 41, 44 47, 53, 116
Rolls Royce 137, 147
Roskill Commission 46
Rownhams, Hampshire 85
Royal Automobile Club 54, 106, 118
Royal Commission on Environmental Pollution (1971) 24

Safety:
air 145-146
road 53, 62-68, 123-125
Sandels, Professor Stina 60
Scott, Peter 139
Shell 26, 34
Ships 27, 31-36
Singer, Professor H. W. 179
Smith, Maurice Temple 195
Society of Motor Manufacturers and Traders 53, 106
Standard of living 24, 160
Standard Oil of New Jersey 26
Stokes, Lord 40, 68
Stonehenge 88
Subsidies:
air 127-135, 140, 146-150, 157, 168
road 42-43, 70, 100-101
general 22, 169
Suburbs 75-77, 84, 91, 175, 181, 190
Sunday Times, 49, 187
Supersonic flight 129-132, 150
Survival 18, 182, 184-197

Technology 17, 20-21, 128, 187, 192-195
Technological Exponential 20, 102, 146
Technostructure 21
Telecommunications 192, 193

Y

—